AF479386

PERSONA

MODELS AT HOME BY

HADLEY HUDSON

HATJE CANTZ

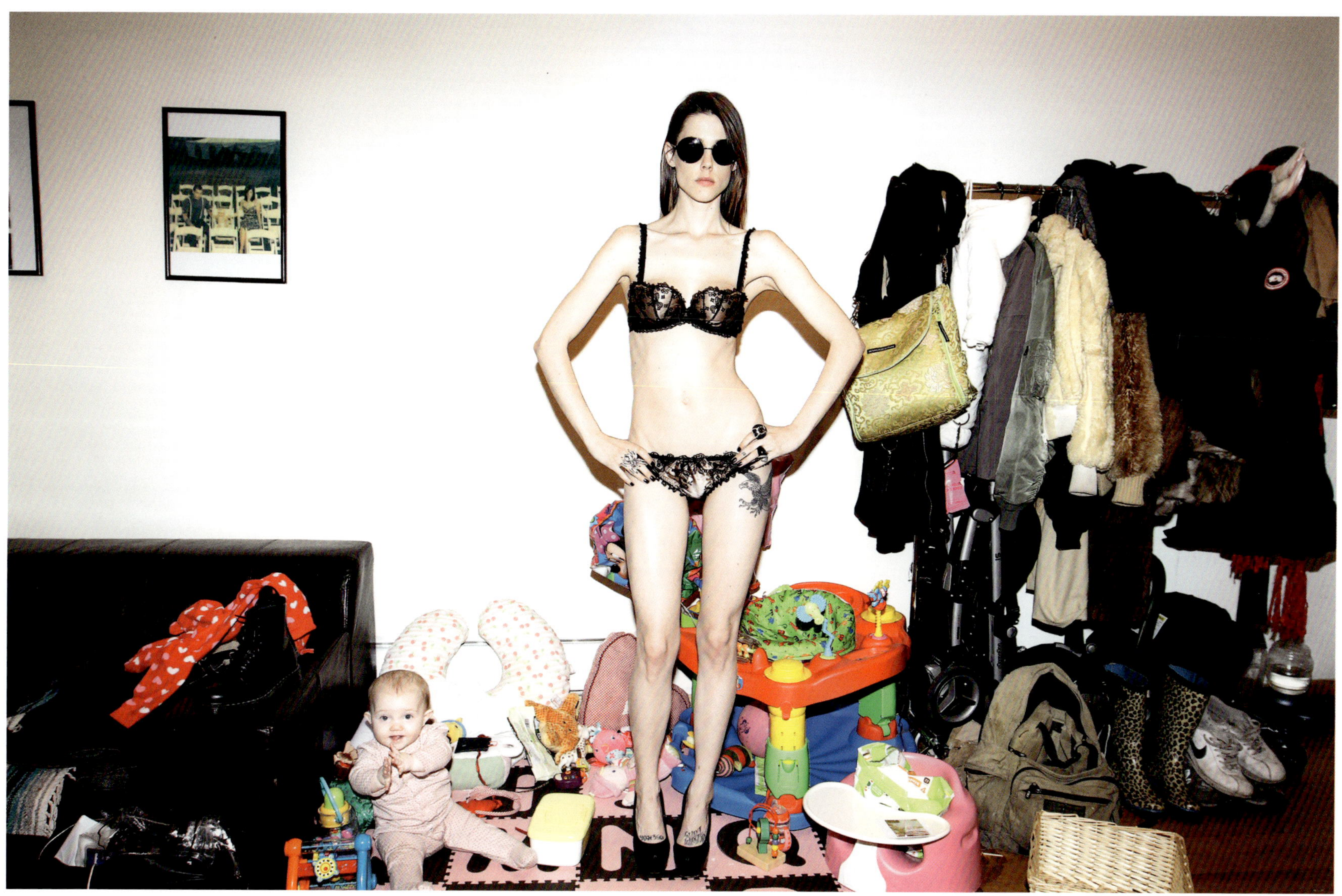

Raquel, 2008
Paris

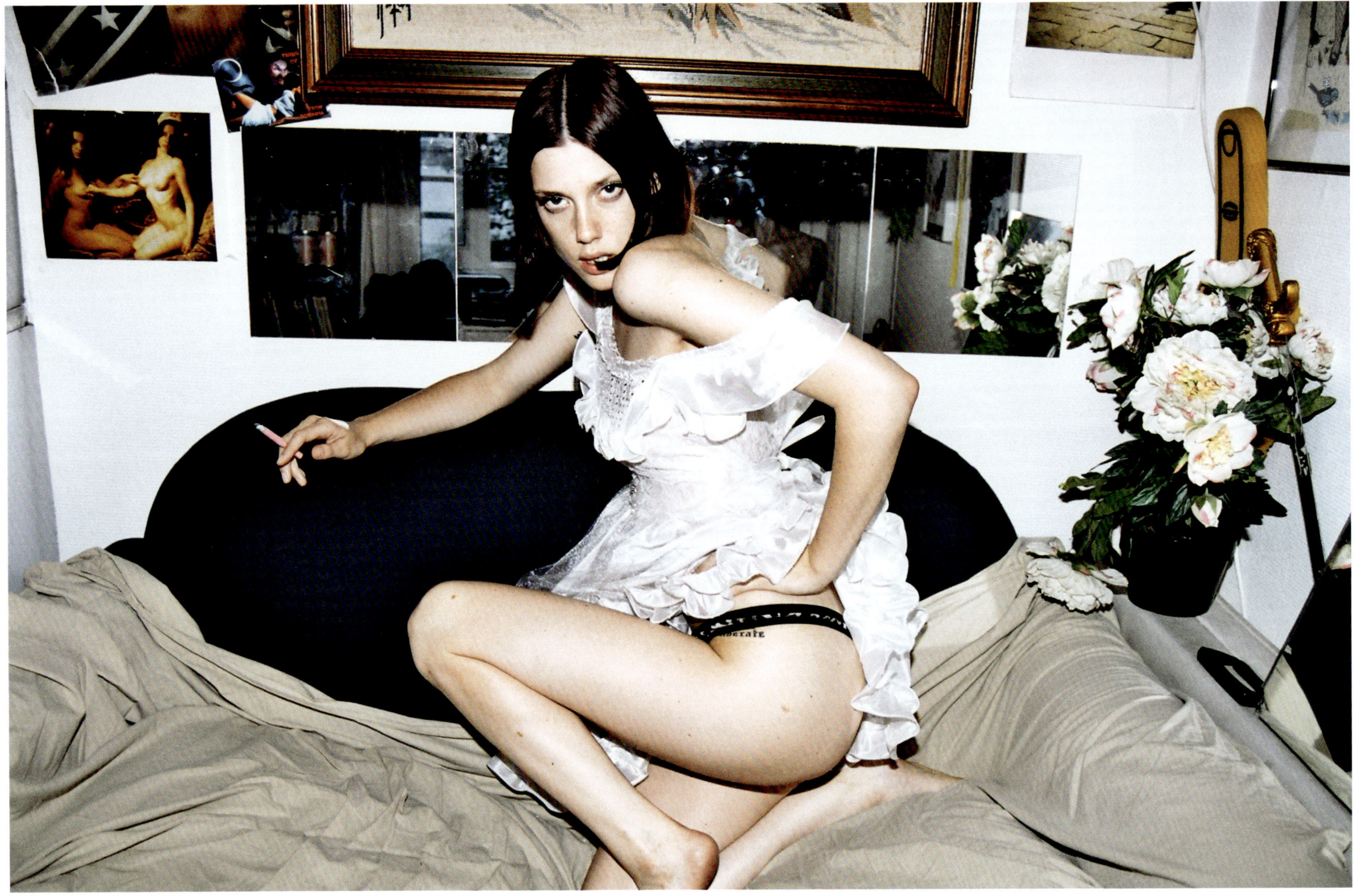

"Sometimes I think all my pictures are just pictures of me.
My concern is the human predicament; only what I consider
the human predicament may simply be my own."
Richard Avedon

In 2014, I went looking for the perfect photographer to feature in the opening pages of a new book about the makers of fashion images. I'd met Hadley Hudson a few years earlier, when she shot a portrait of me for an arty magazine, and had followed her work, shooting aspiring fashion models in their own clothes in their own homes, ever since. Hudson's pictures were compelling and very much of their time: more documentary than fantasy, rendered in harshly-lit snapshot style, sexy not only because they featured beautiful young people, but also because they seemed awkward, intimate, knowing, and loving. They offered glimpses of what a lover would see, of real people, not manufactured images. Though she shot with a digital camera, that great facilitator of artificiality, her work felt authentic.

When she took her first model-at-home picture in 2008, Hadley has told me, she was shocked by the difference between shooting a model on a set for a client, and a girl or a boy in their own clothes, in their own environment. "I realized that I was prone to extreme projection on models, surely an effect of their extreme beauty," she told me. "I was projecting some fantasy upon them which had nothing to do with them." That's what fashion photography does. Or rather, what it has always done. Nowadays, though, it's changing, pushed to reinvent itself by social media, a worldwide flood of selfies, and the new anyone-can-do-it ethic that's caused an existential crisis in the genre.

Fashion, stripped to its bare essence, is about change. Hudson's work reflects those changes, even as it builds on the century of fashion imagery that preceded her, and helps invents its future. In Persona, Hudson has collected the best of the images she's shot over the last eight years of sessions with more than a hundred models in more than a hundred locations. The models' homes range from posh apartments to rooms in their parents' houses, to squats to the often even more squalid apartments where agencies warehouse the endless parade of wannabe "faces" awaiting their moment in the glare of fashion's strobe.

We can still project onto these kids (for that's what they are), but in Hudson's pictures they project back, revealing tenderness, cockiness, fear, ambition, self-interest, and their willingness to both use and be used in return for rewards that may never come, and may prove quite a bit less than expected if and when they do. For Hadley Hudson, the reward comes in clicking the shutter. Thanks to her, we can all share the revelation of what's behind the model's mask, the designer's frock, or the hair and makeup artist's wizardry. There, buried under the personas, are personalities being born.

— Michael Gross, author of *Focus: The Secret, Sexy, Sometimes Sordid World of Fashion Photographers, Model: The Ugly Business of Beautiful Women,* and other books.

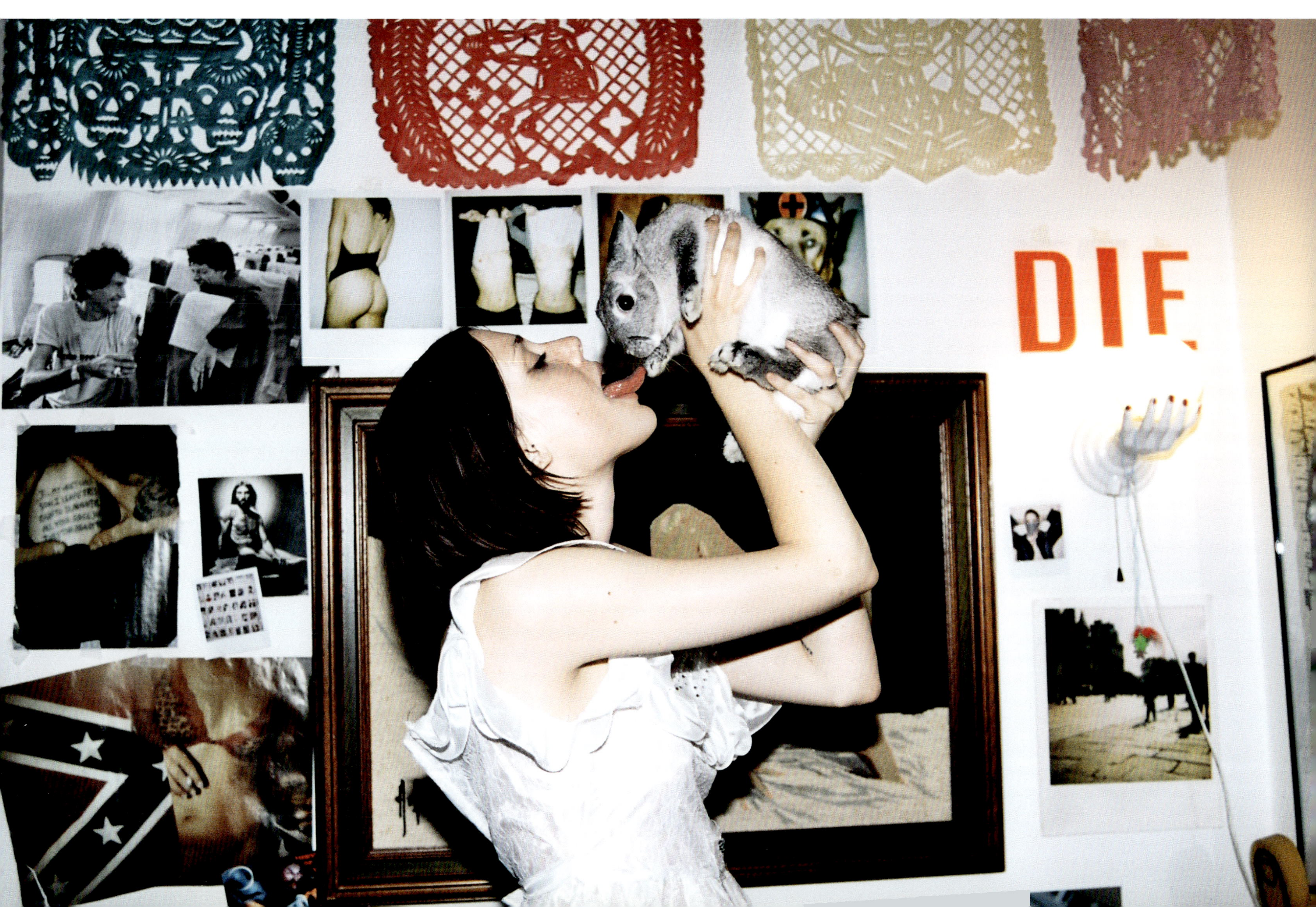

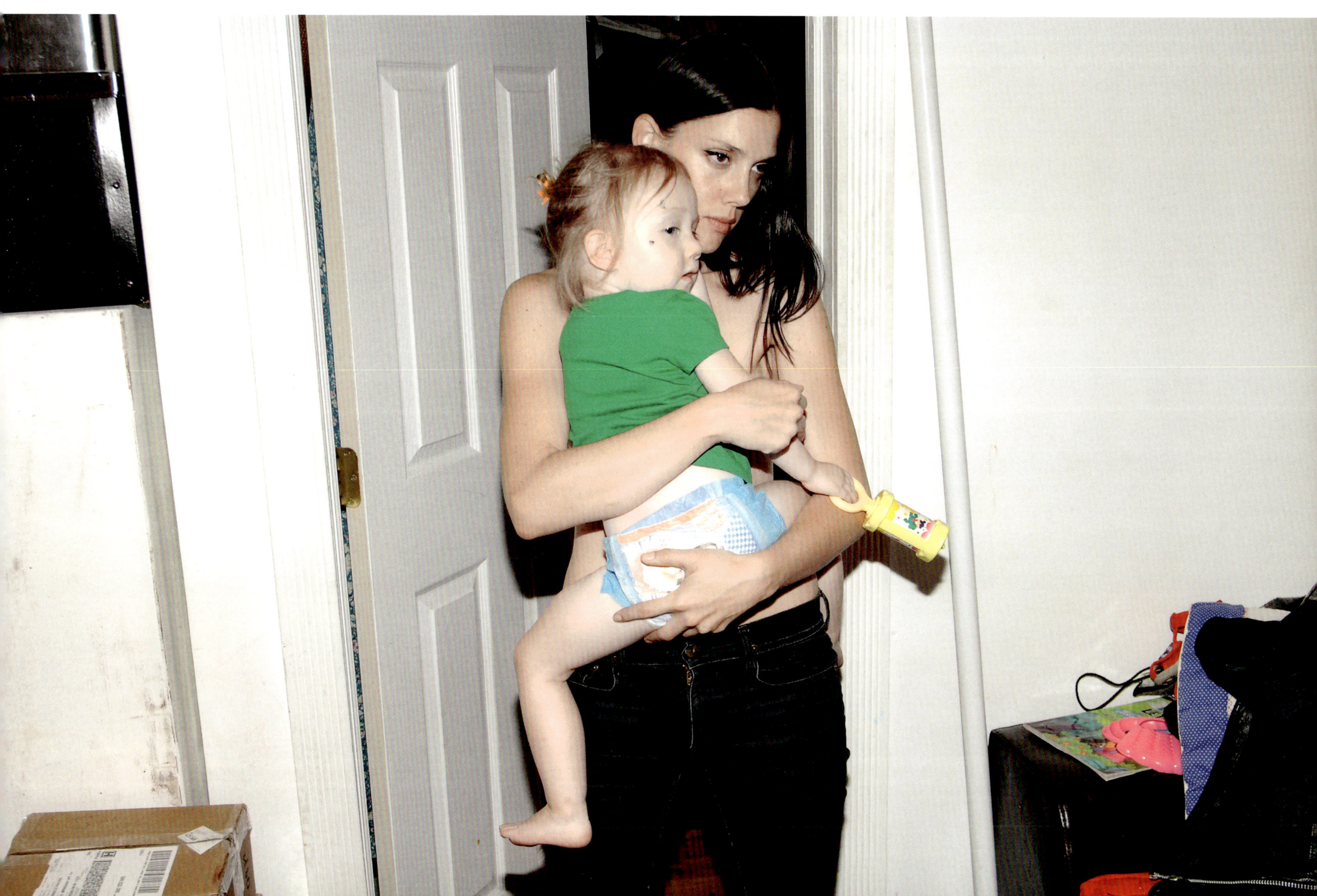

Micky Ayoub, 2011
St. Marks Place, New York City

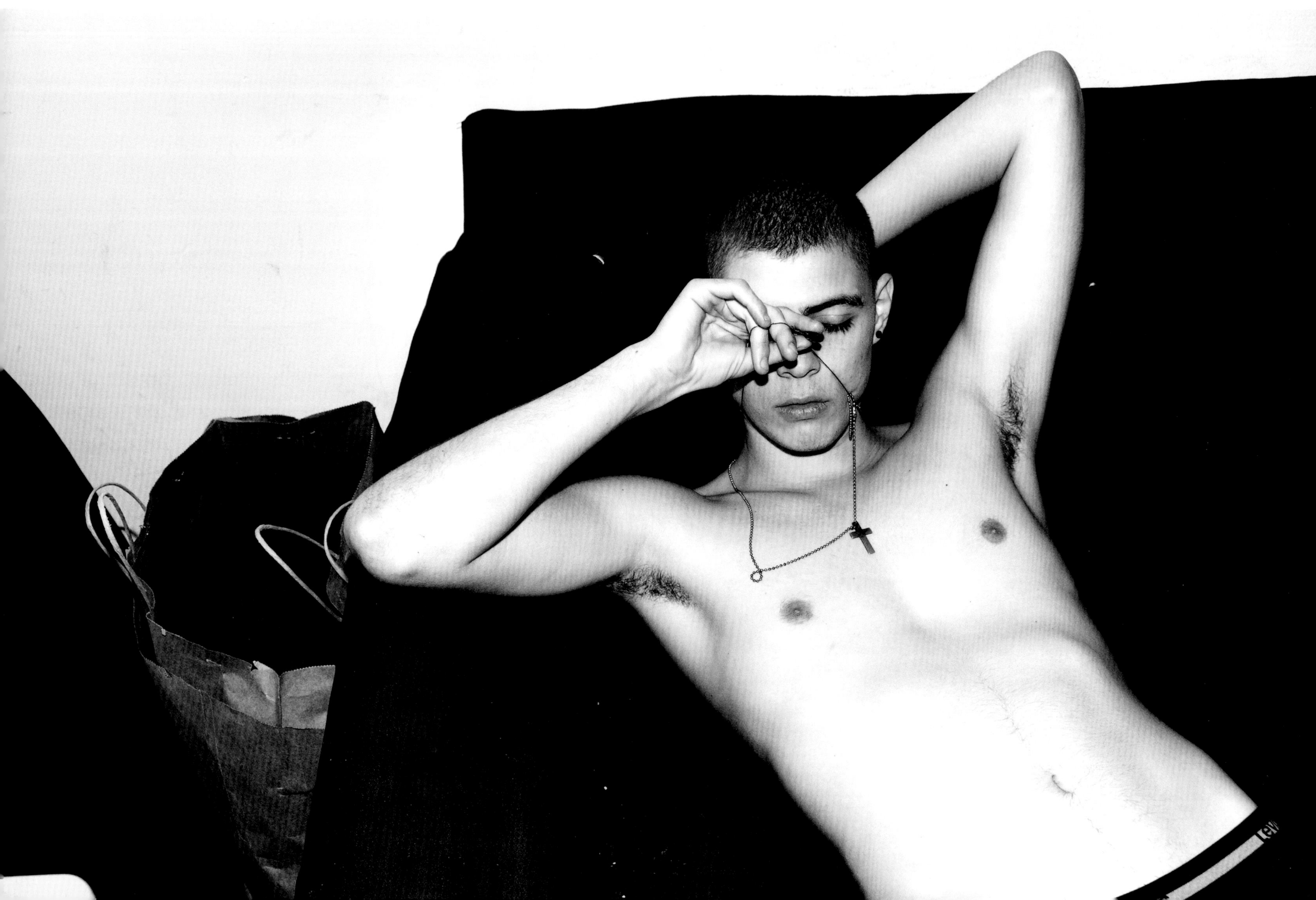

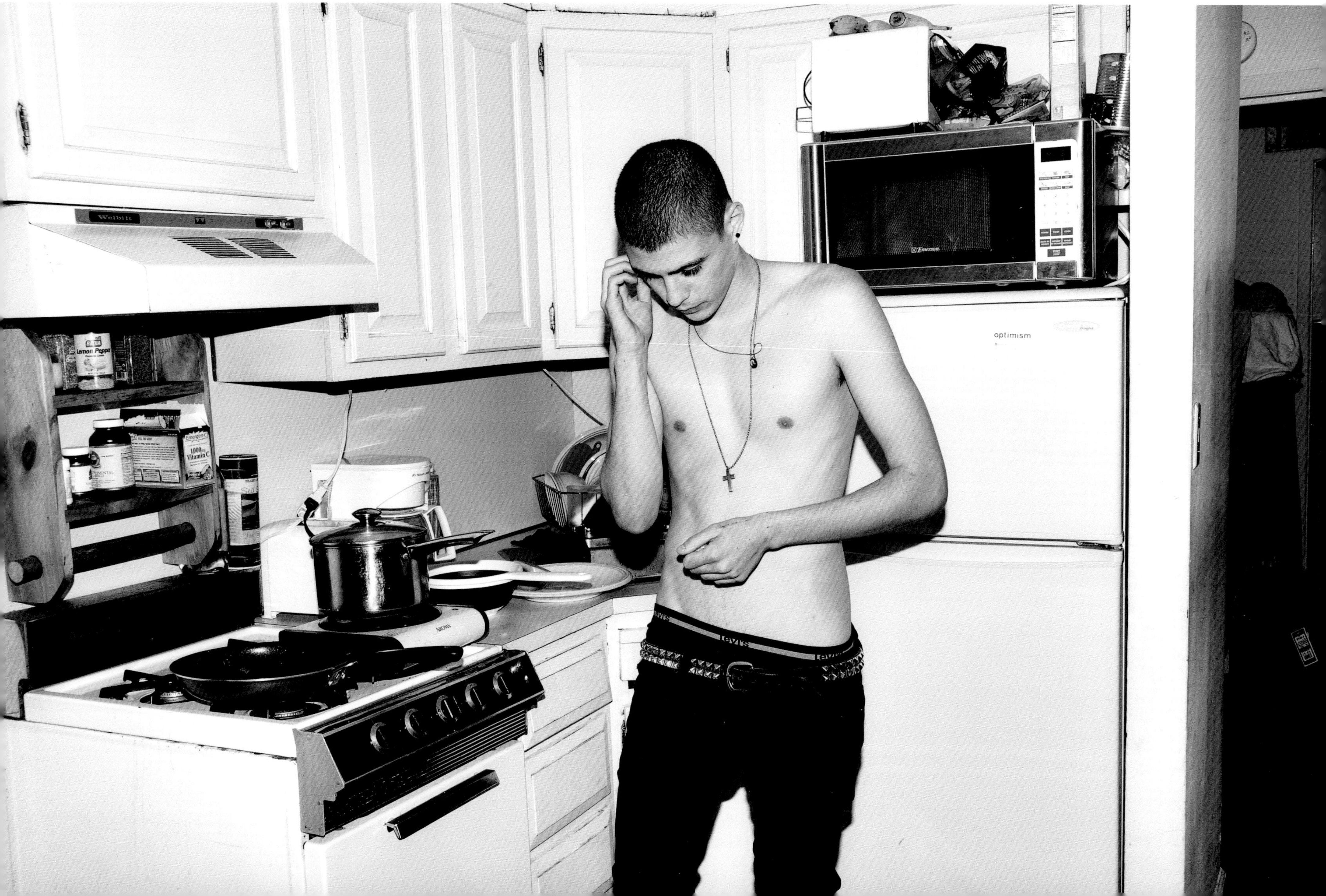

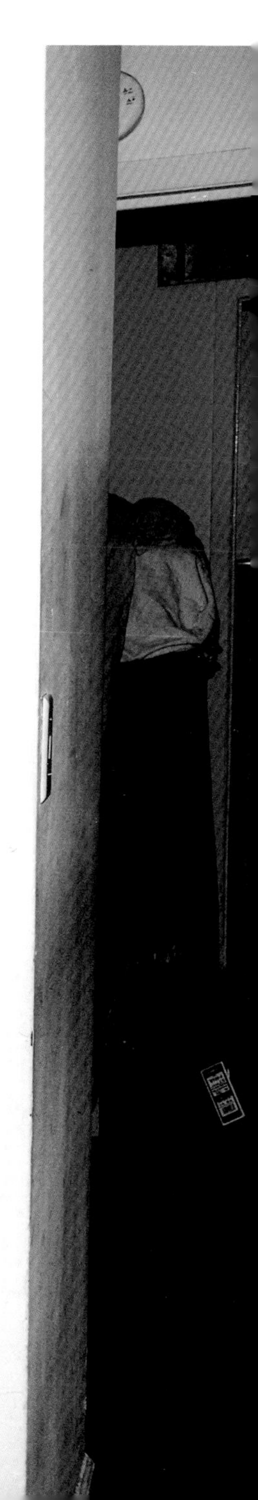

Priscilla after the break in, 2008
Paris

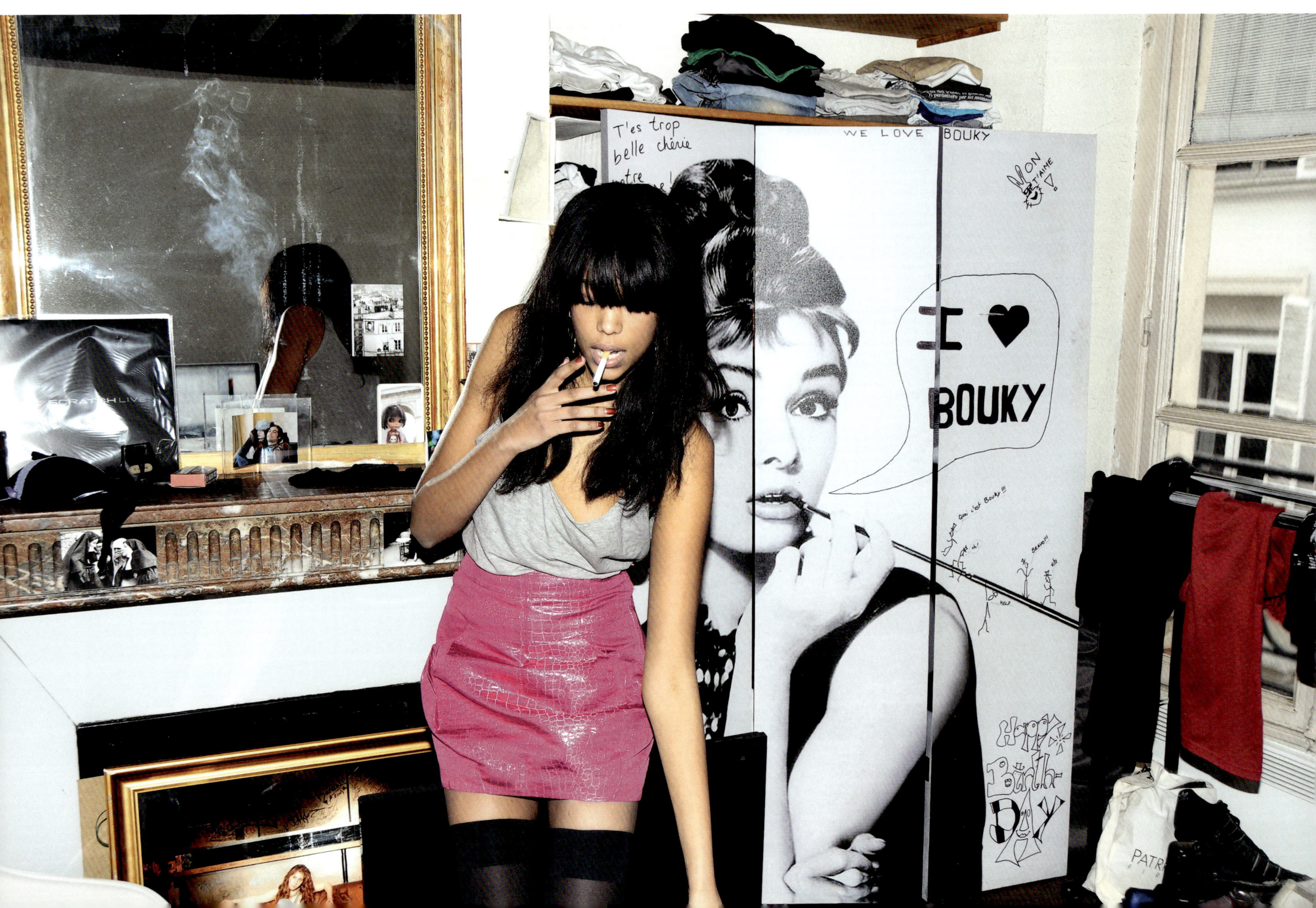

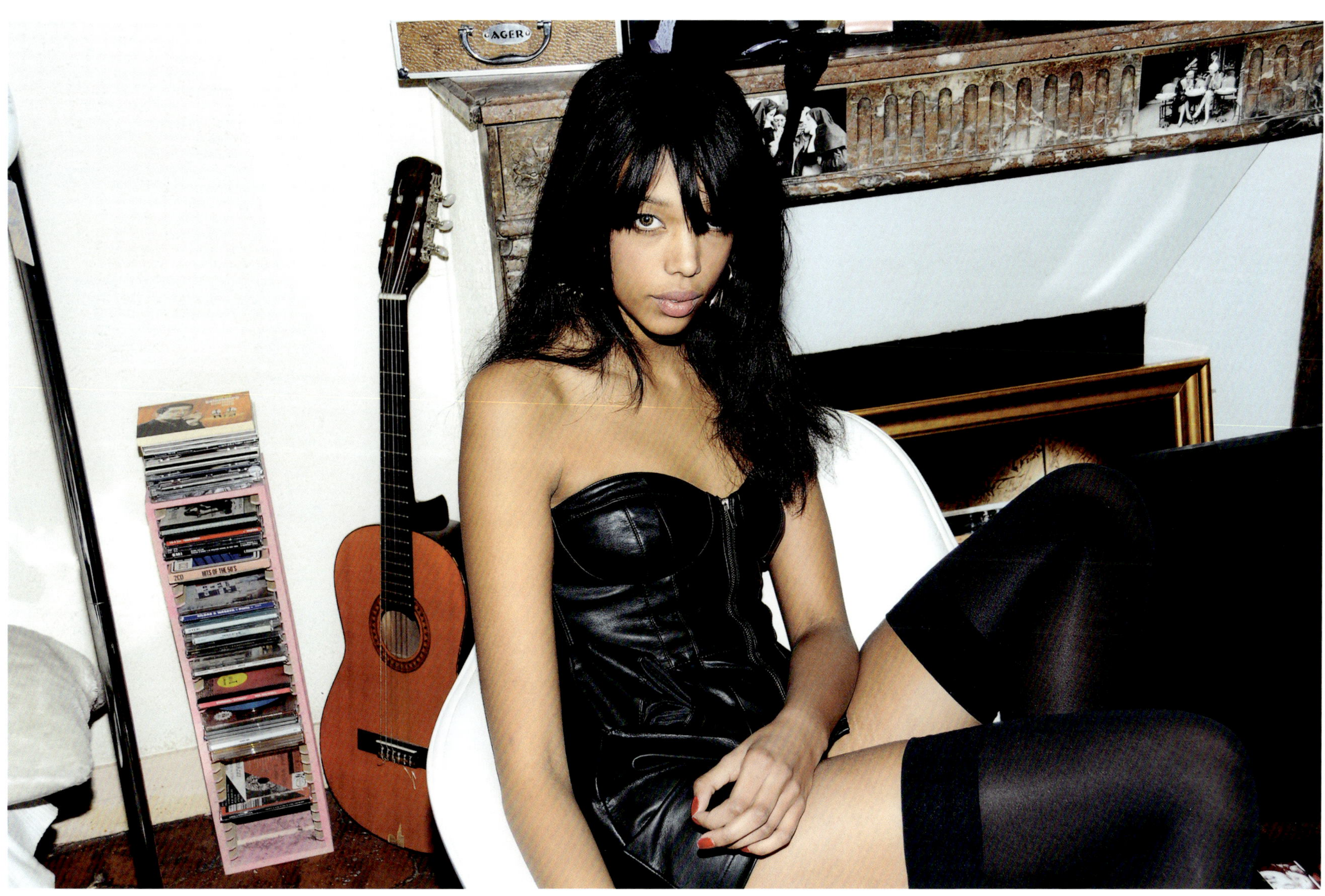

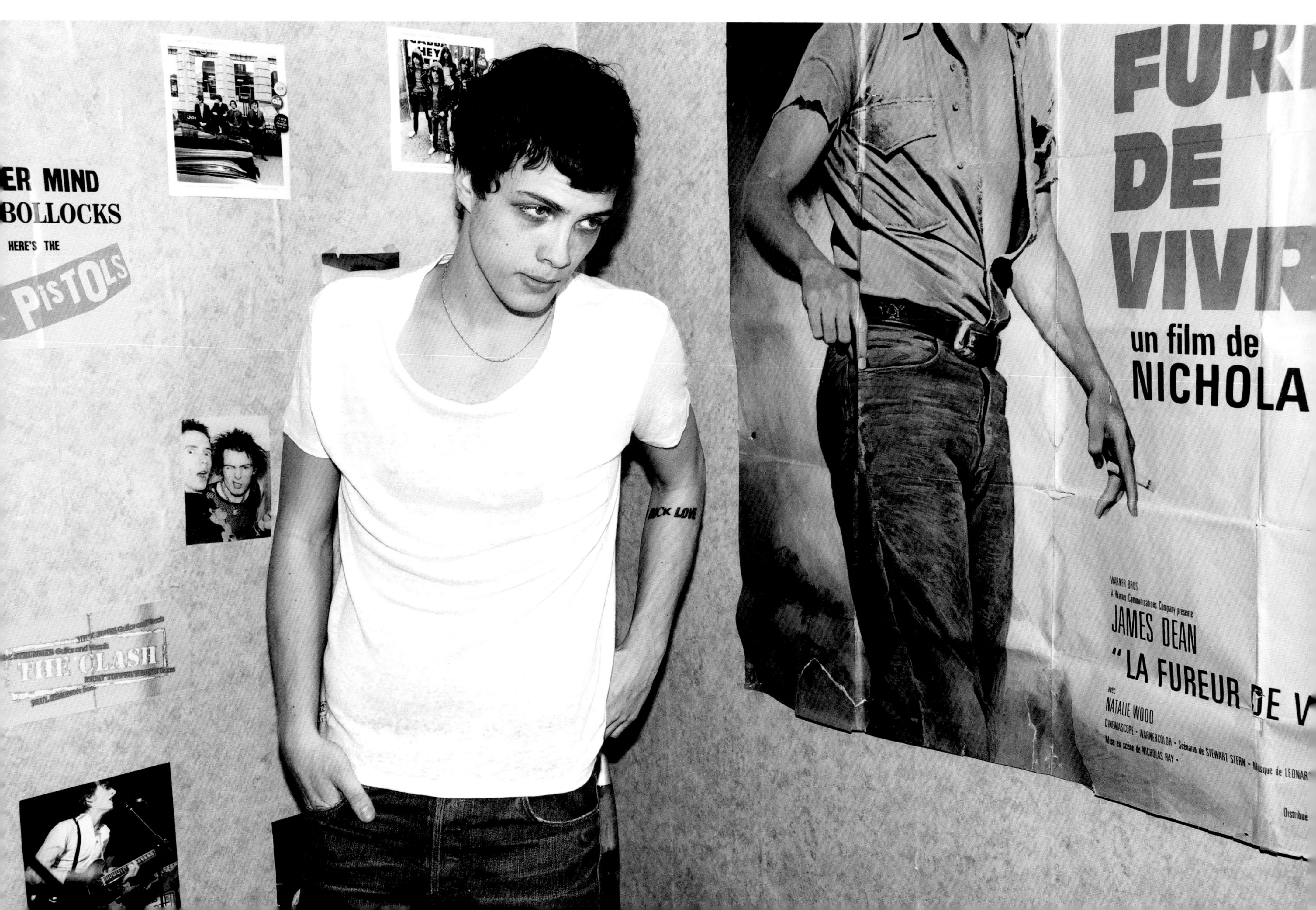
ER MIND
BOLLOCKS
HERE'S THE
PiSTOLS
THE CLASH
FUR
DE
VIVR
un film de
NICHOLA
WARNER BROS
A Warner Communications Company présente
JAMES DEAN
"LA FUREUR DE V
avec
NATALIE WOOD
CINEMASCOPE · WARNERCOLOR · Scénario de STEWART STERN · Musique de LEONAR
Mise en scène de NICHOLAS RAY ·
Distribue

 Nico, 2015
Bushwick, New York City

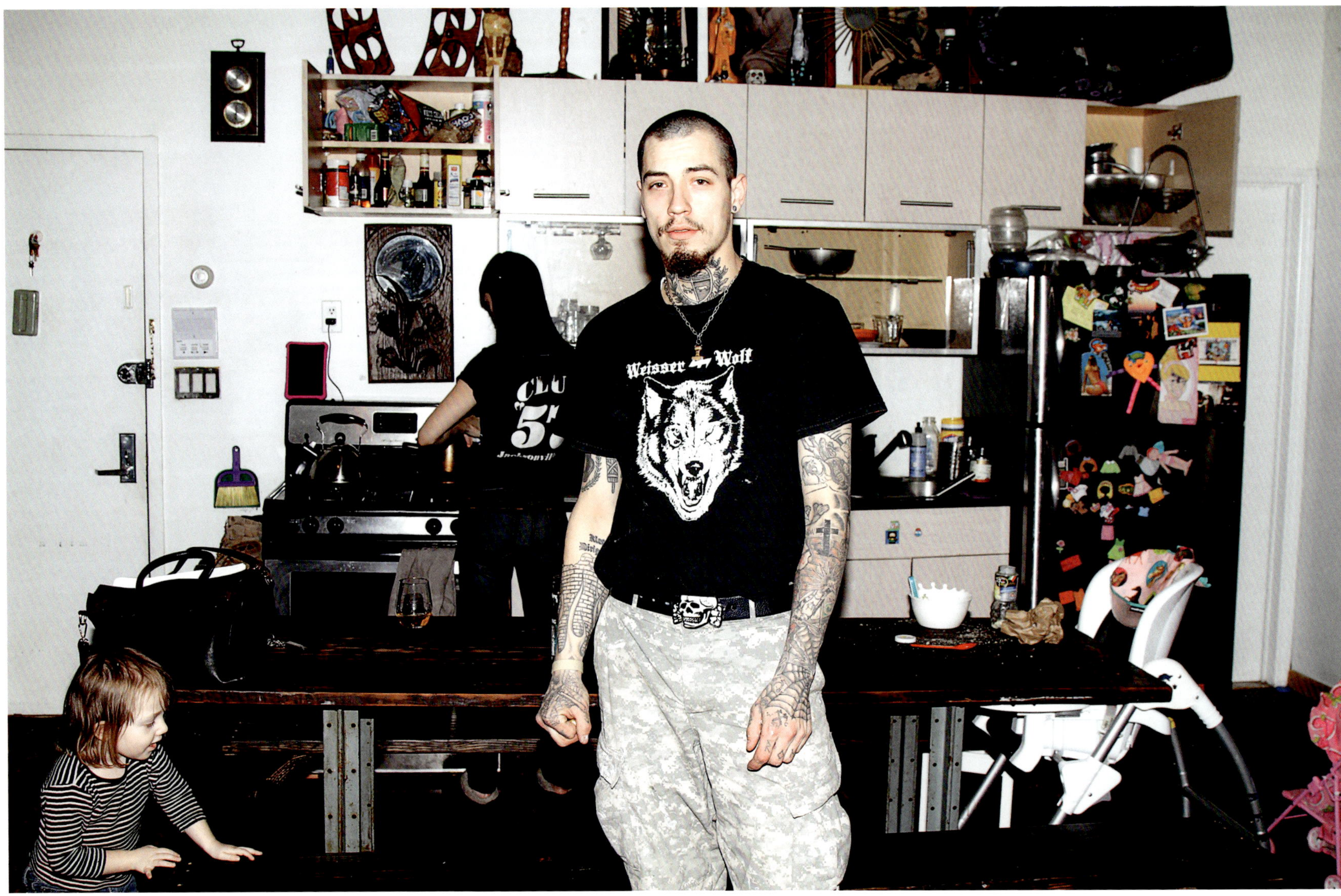

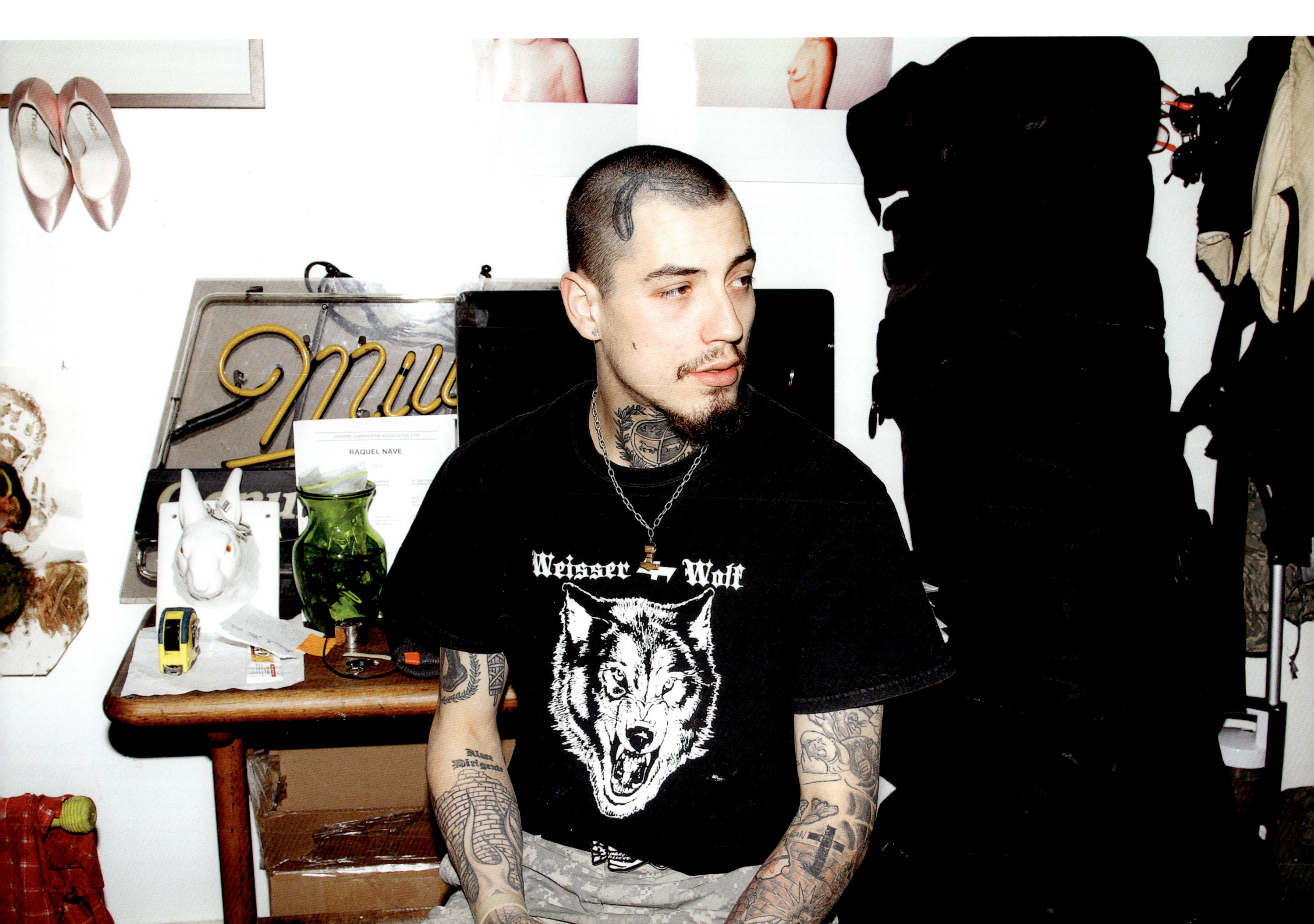

 Rebekah, 2015
Brooklyn, New York City

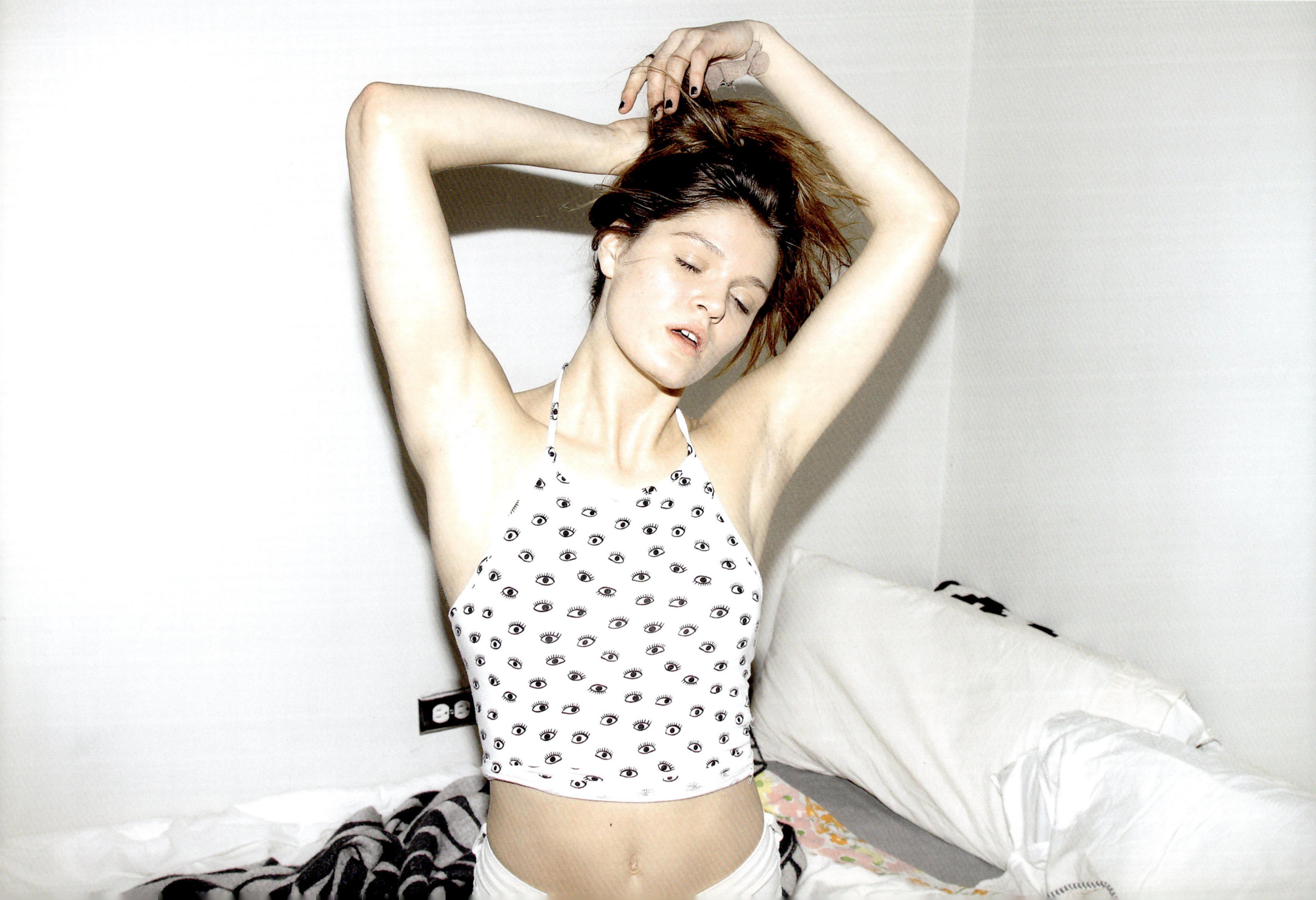

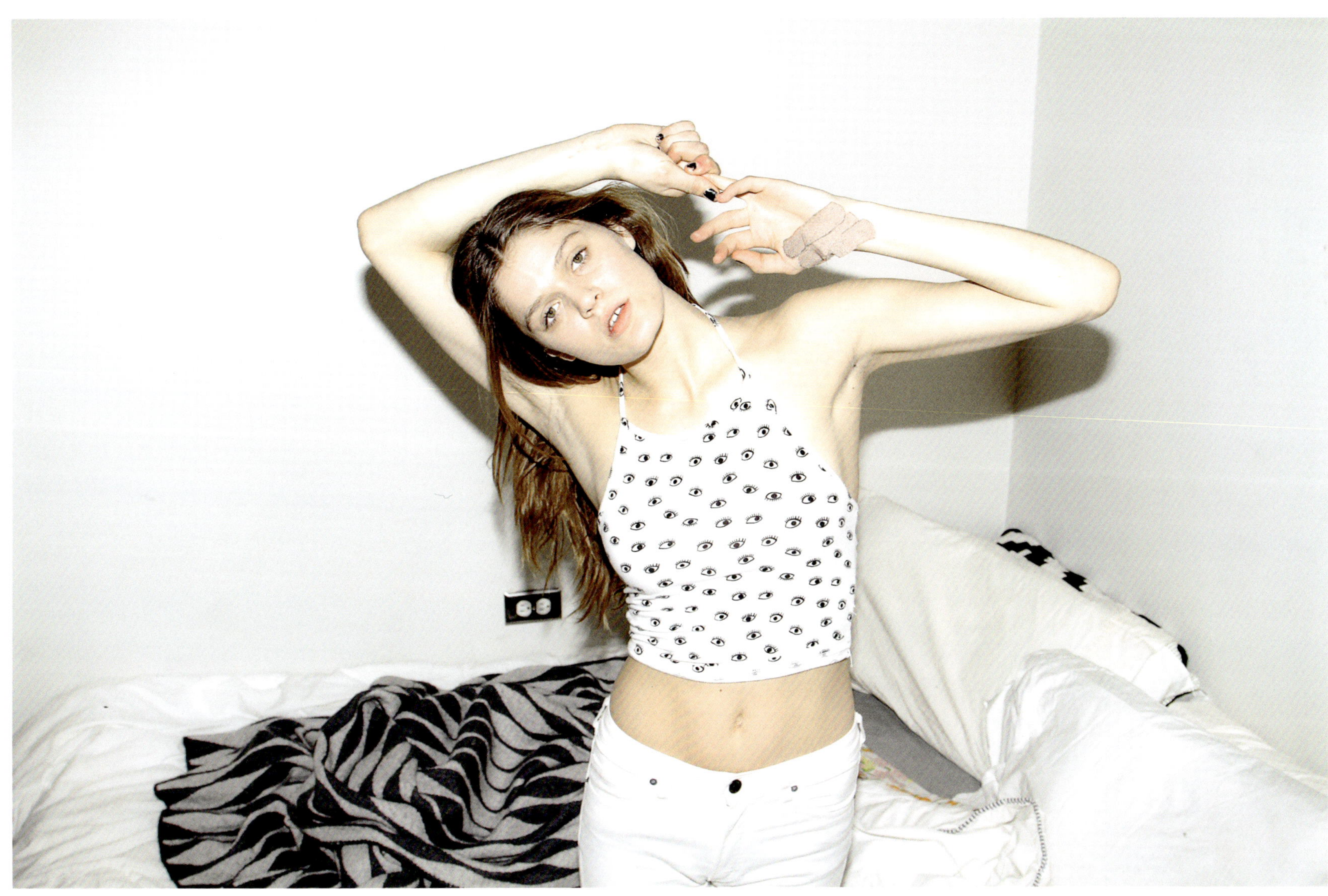

Bushwick, New York City

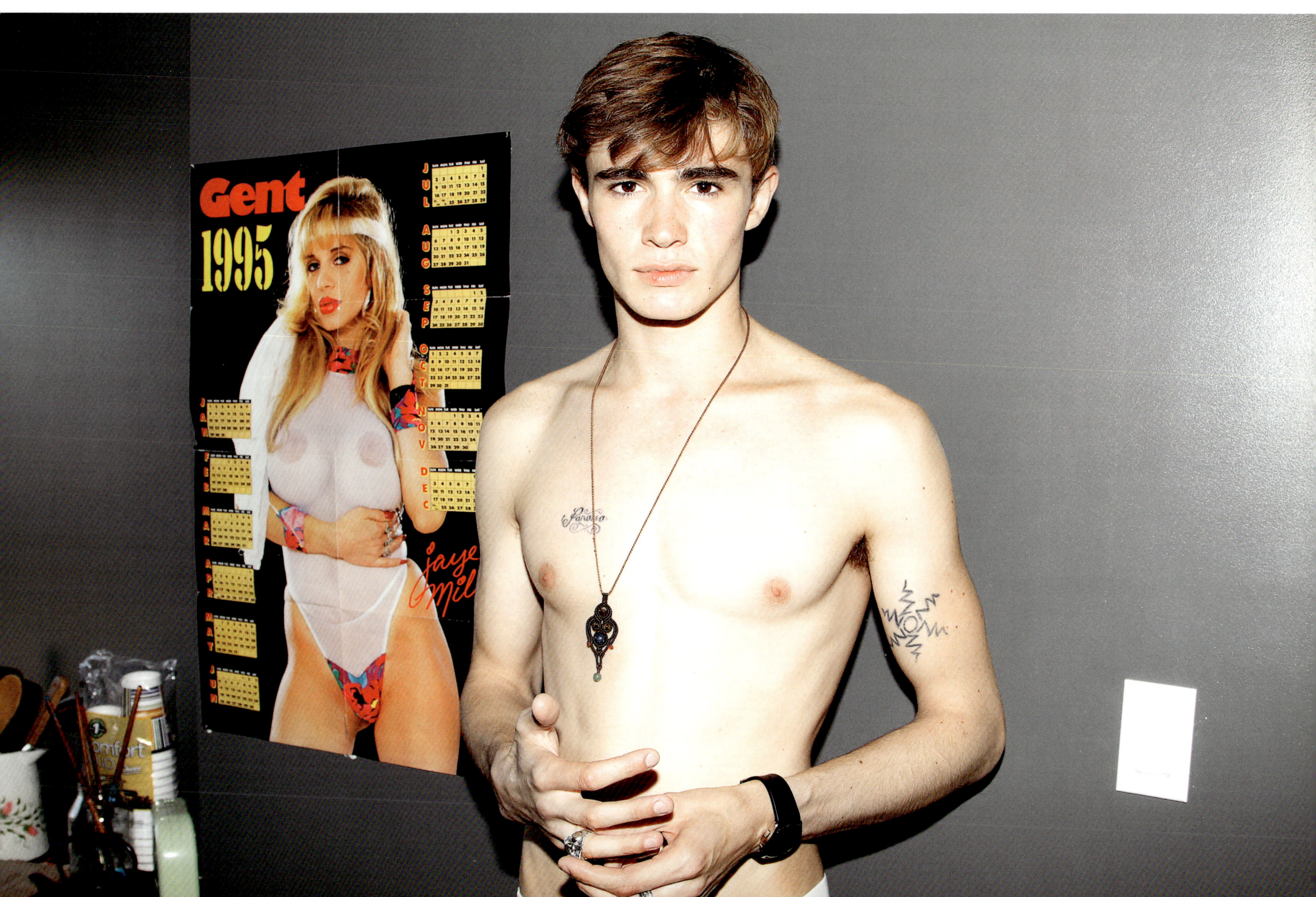

Scott, 2009
Queens, New York City

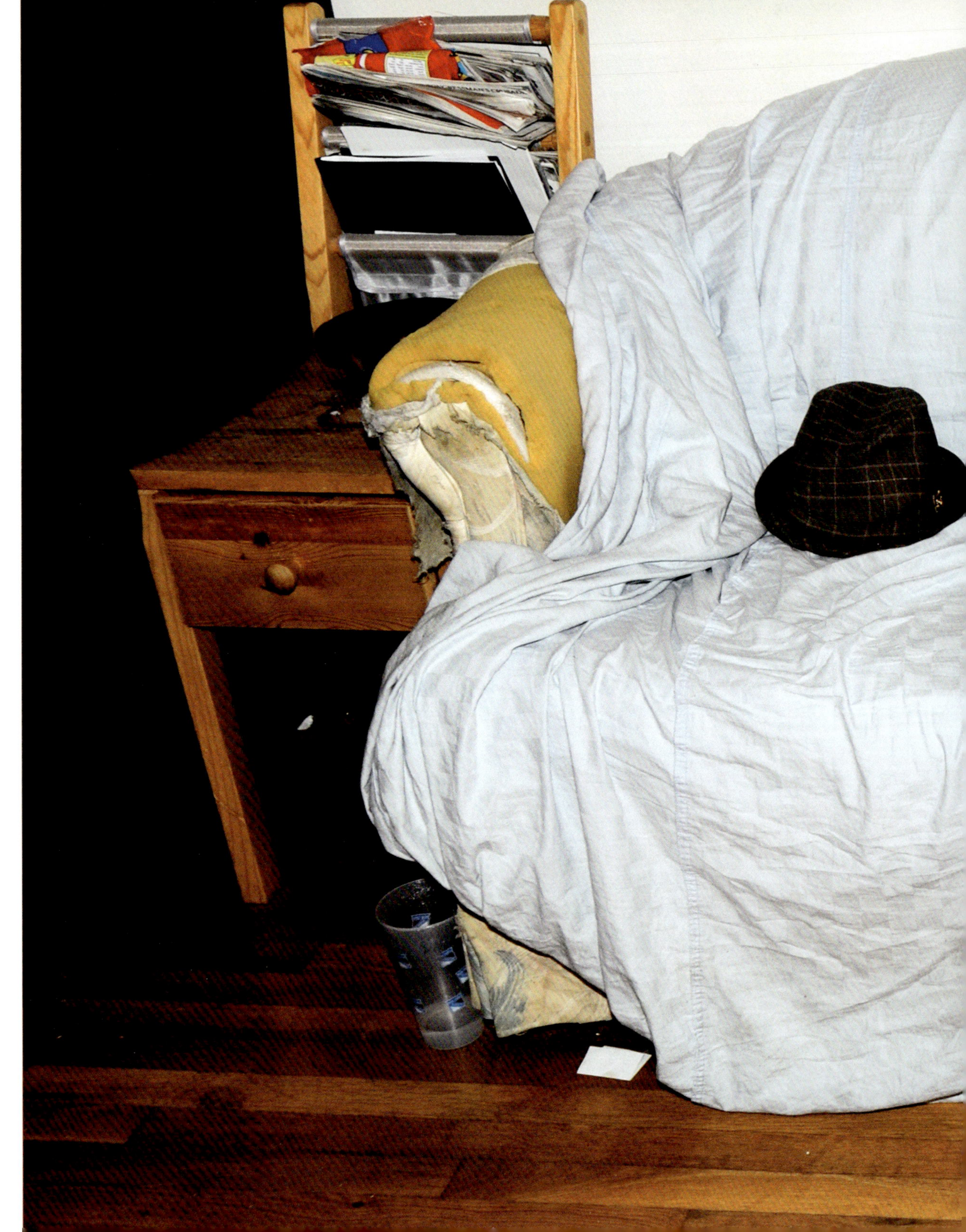

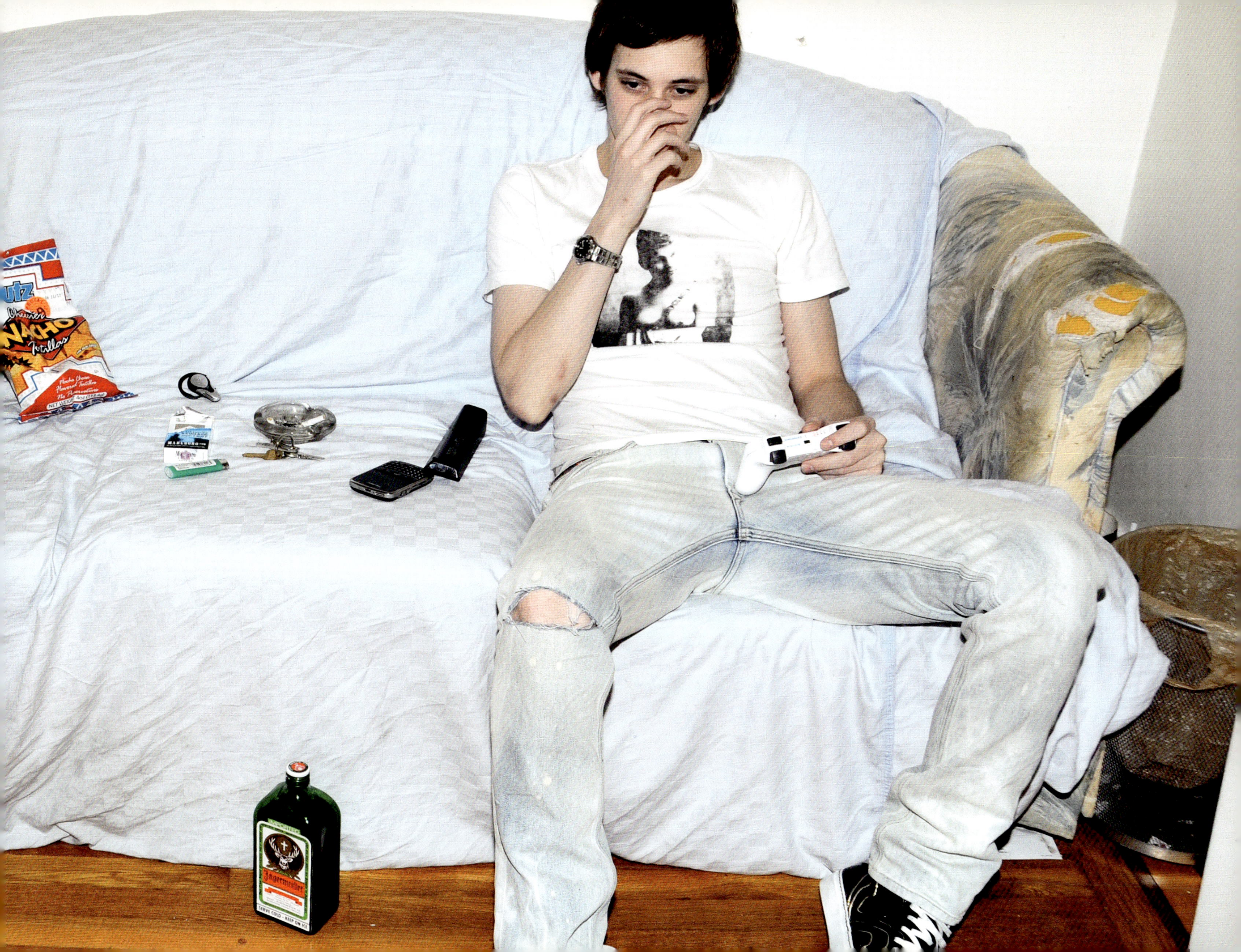

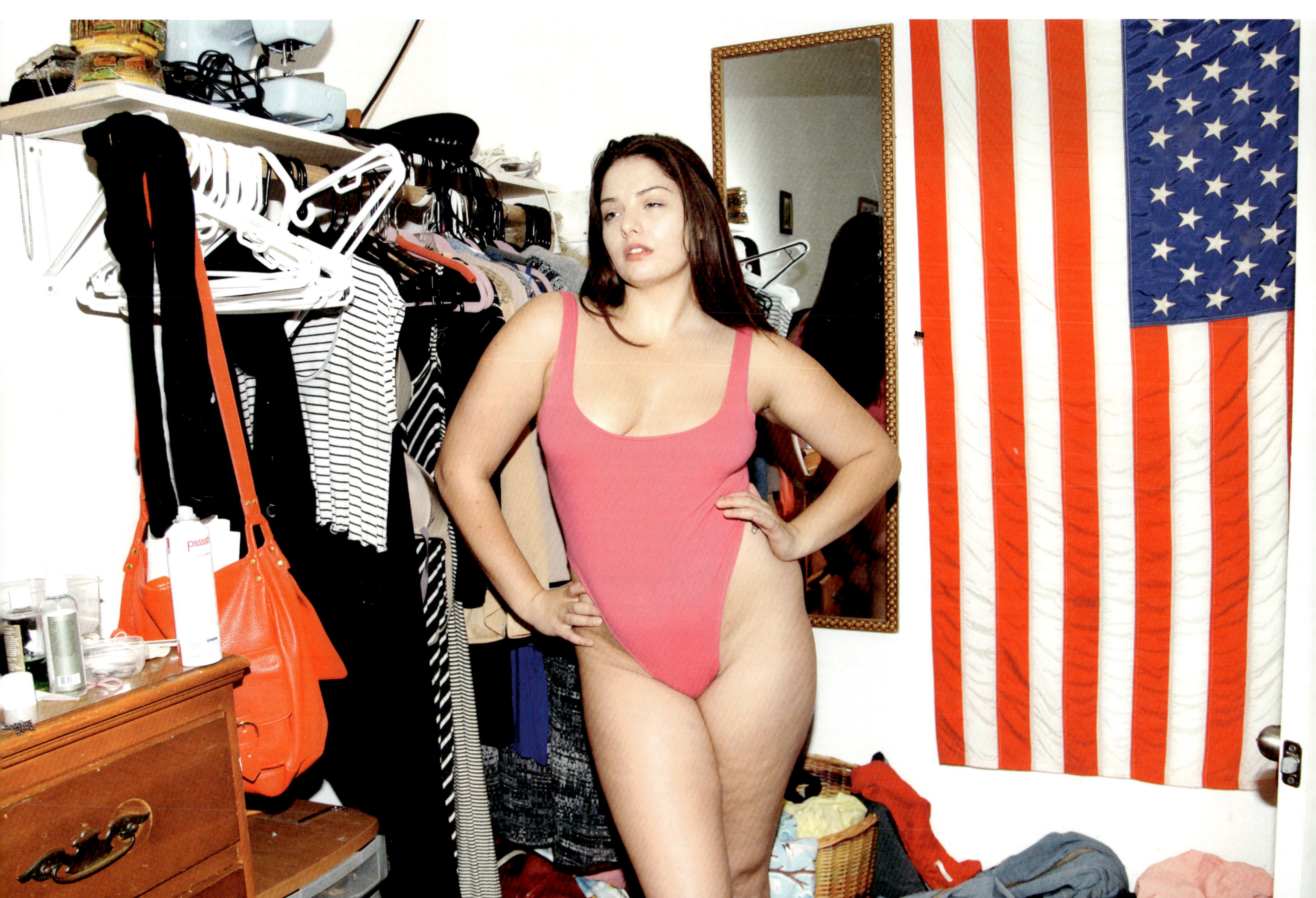

Marcelle, 2013   25
Bushwick, New York City

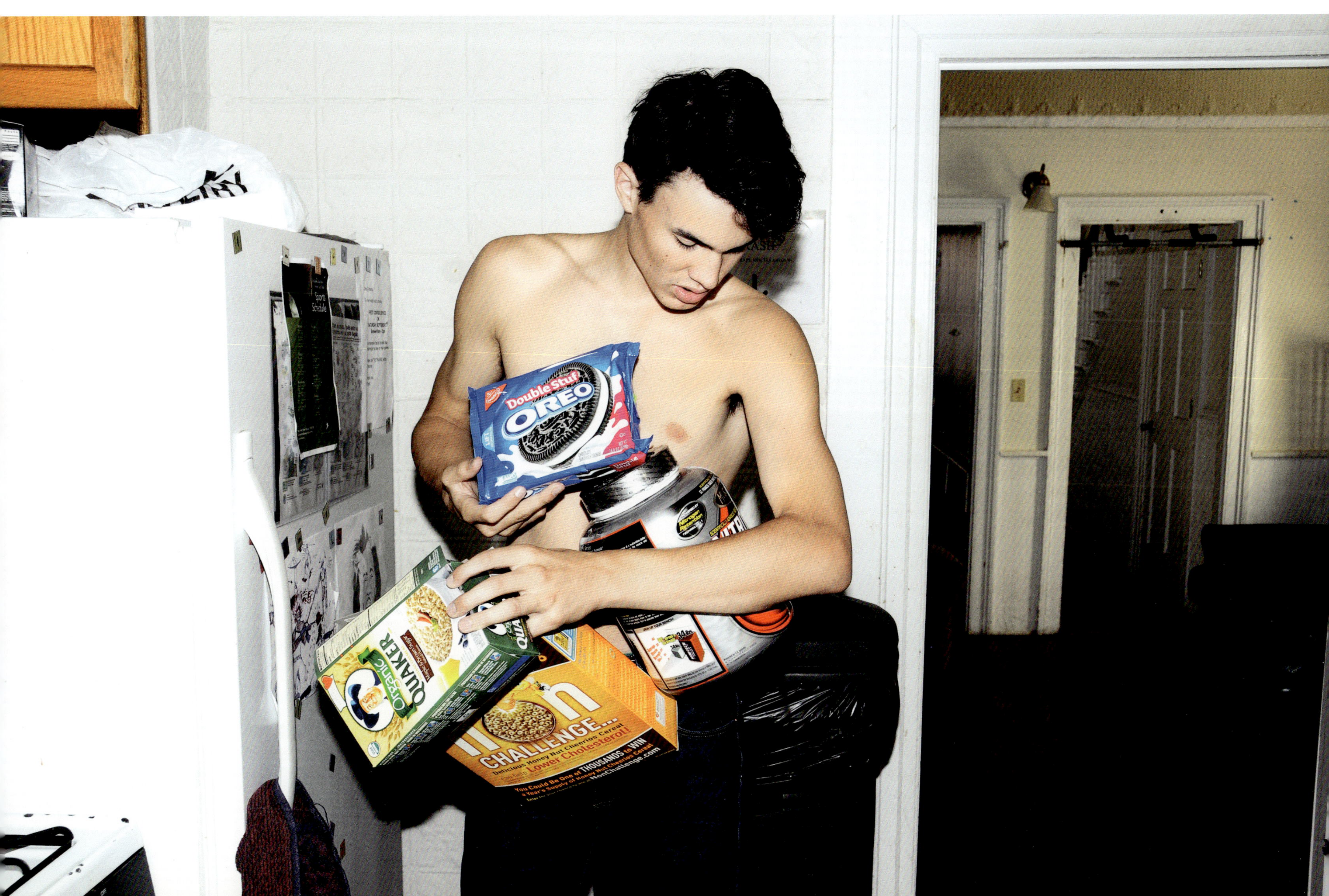
Double Stuf
OREO
QUAKER
ORGANIC
CHALLENGE...
Delicious Honey Nut Cheerios Cereal
Lower Cholesterol!

Model apartment, 2009
Queens, *New York City*

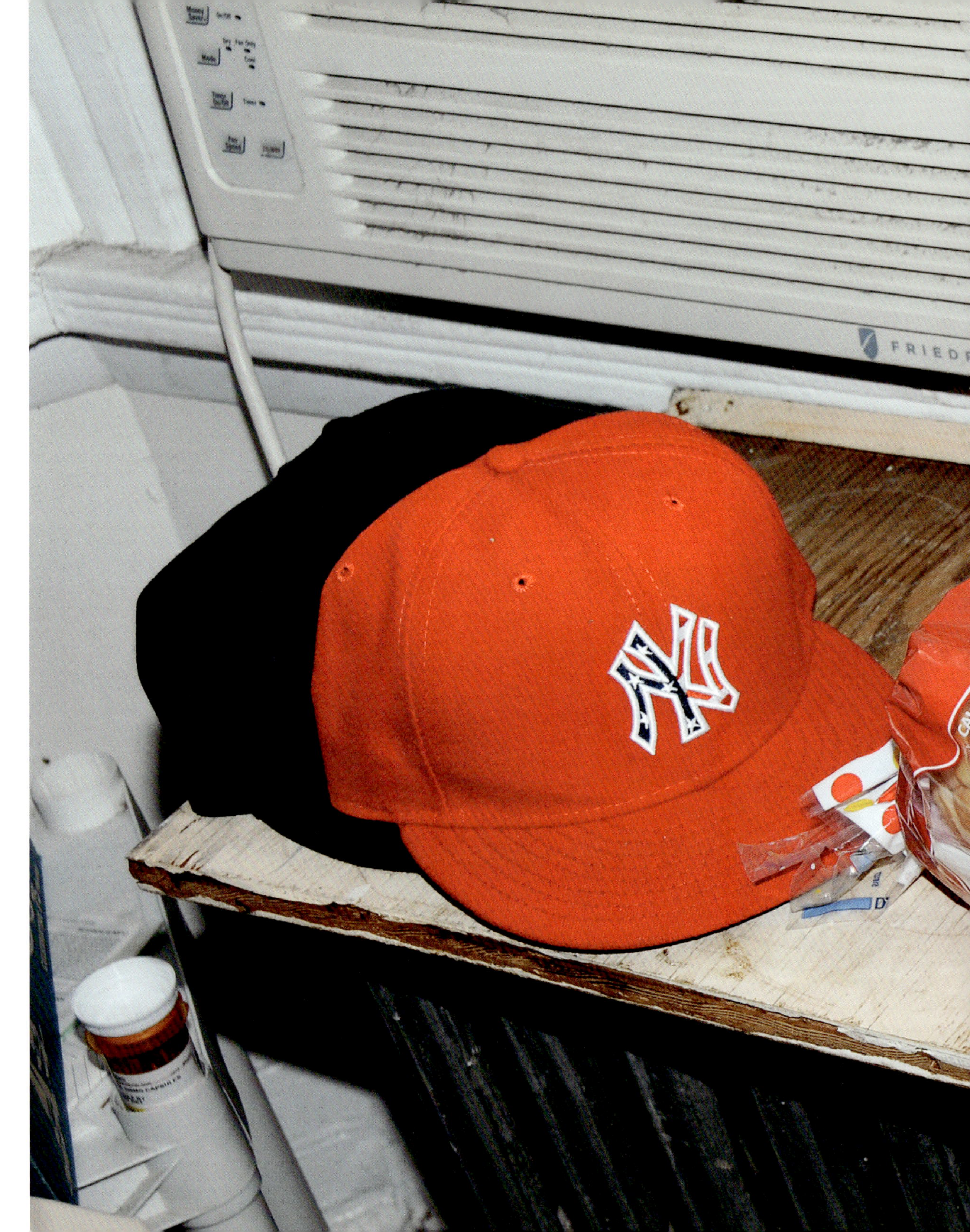

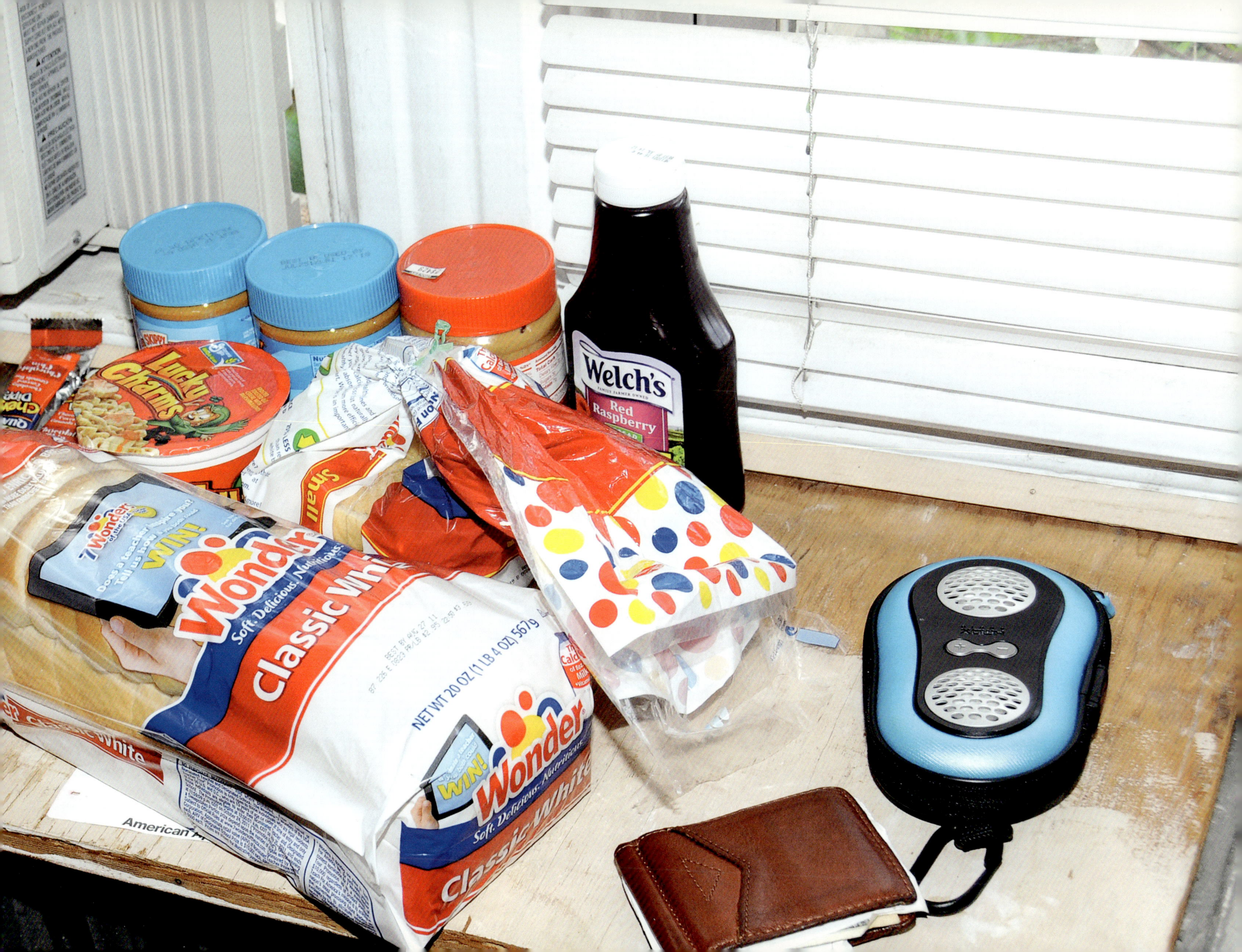

Lucky Charms
Skippy
Wonder
7 Wonder
WIN!
Soft. Delicious. Nutritious.
Classic White
NET WT 20 OZ (1 LB 4 OZ) 567g
Wonder
Classic White
Small
Welch's
FAMILY FARMER OWNED
Red Raspberry
American

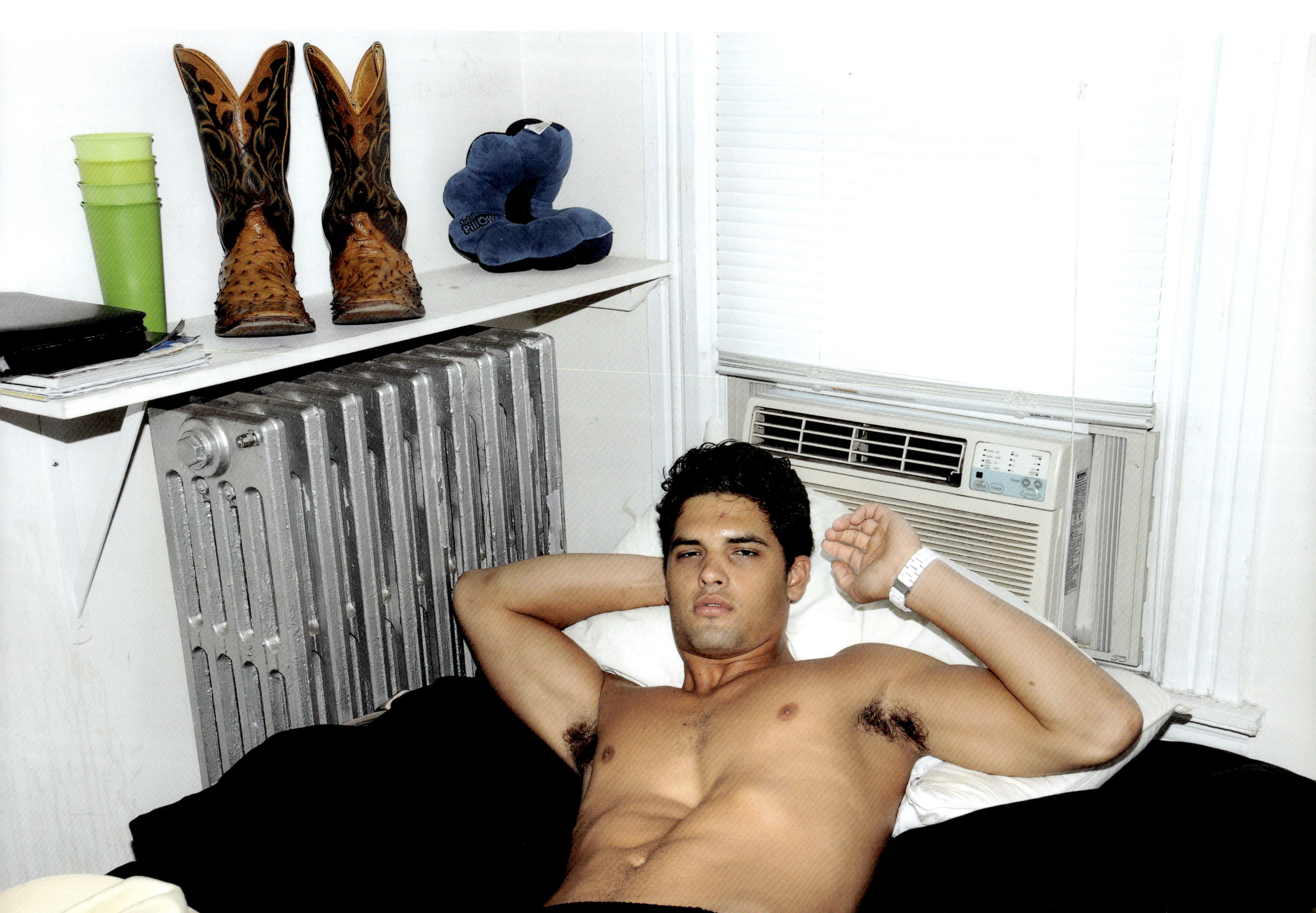

Ben, 2014
East Village, New York City

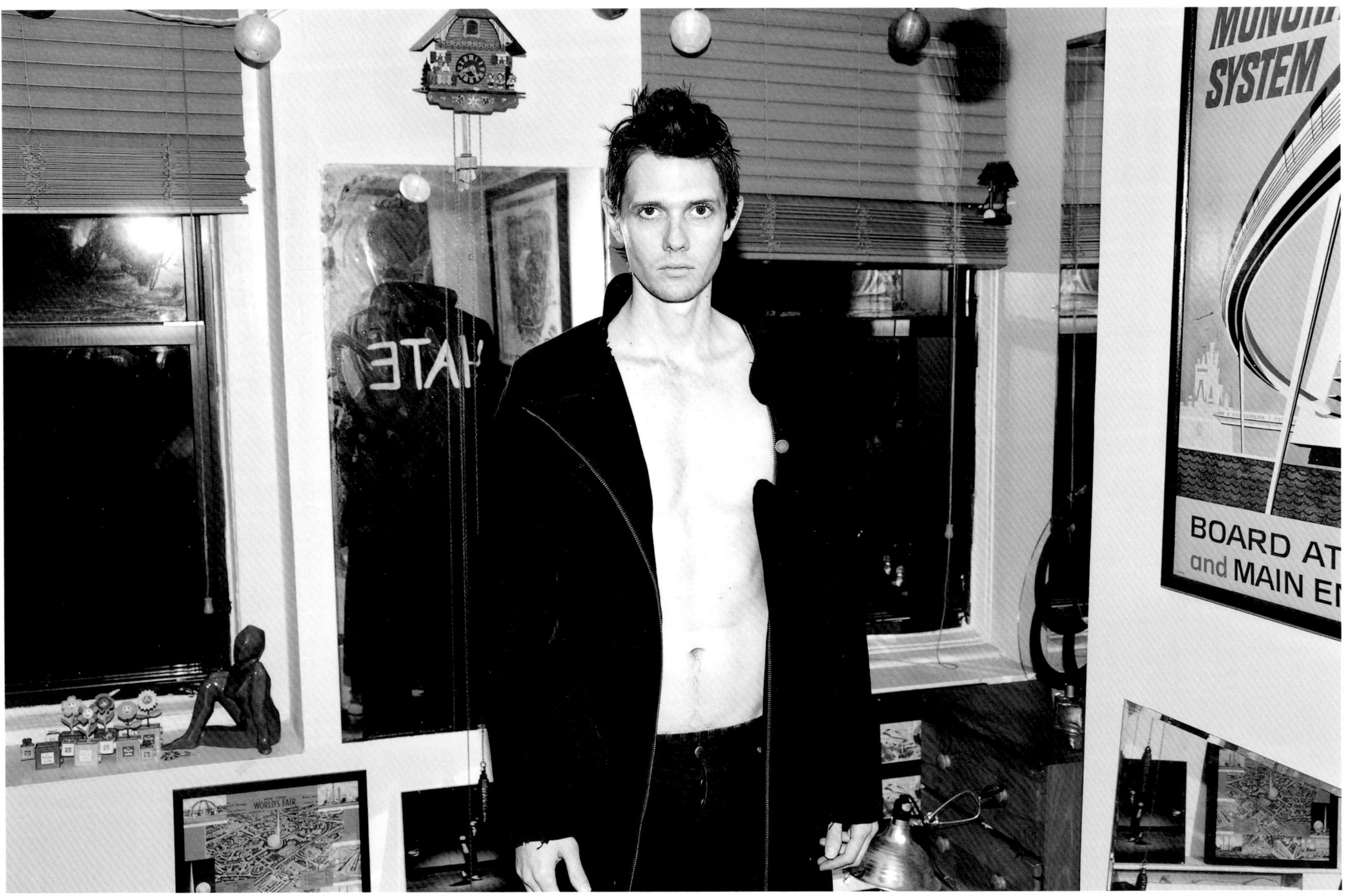

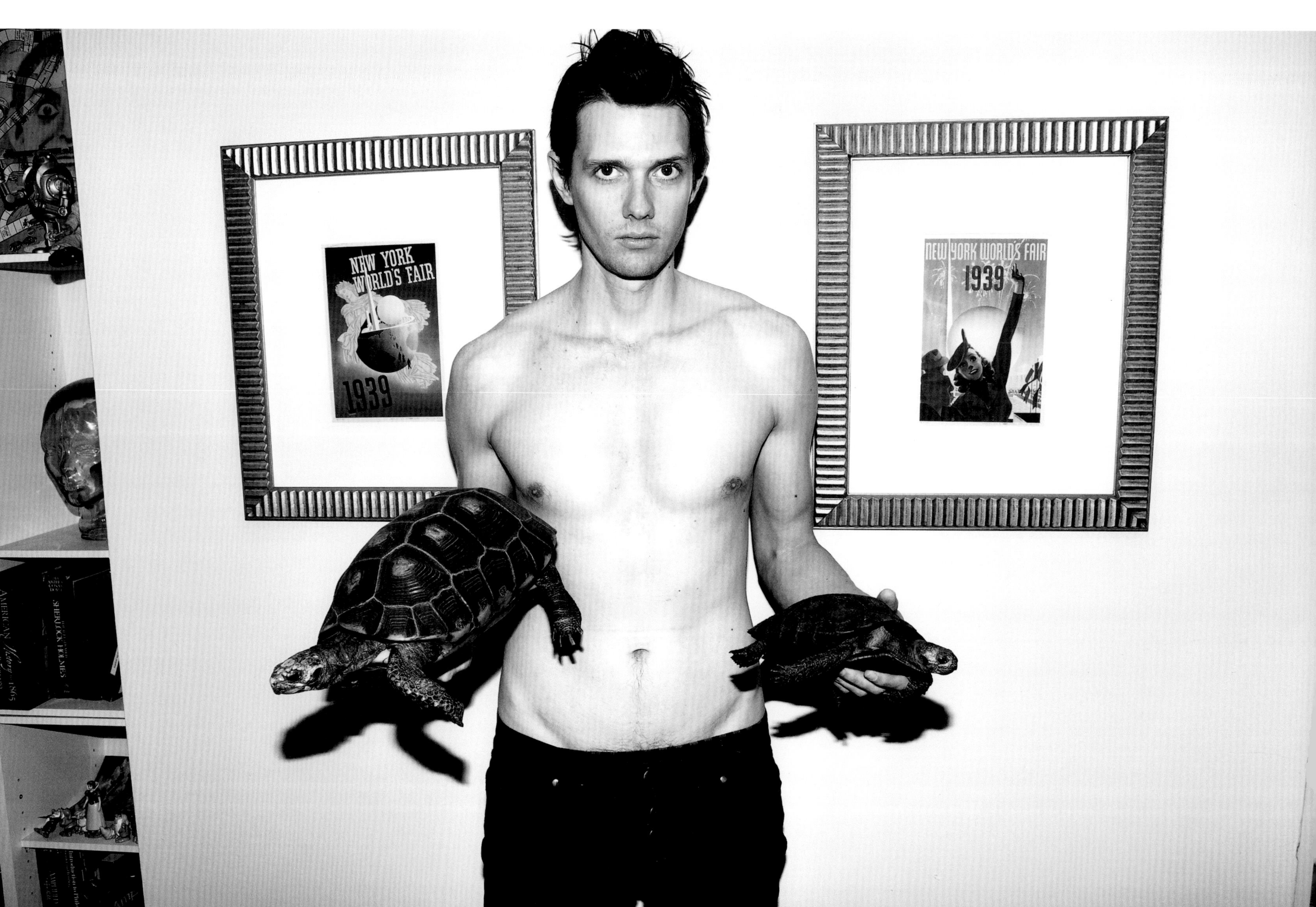
NEW YORK
WORLD'S FAIR
1939

NEW YORK WORLD'S FAIR
1939

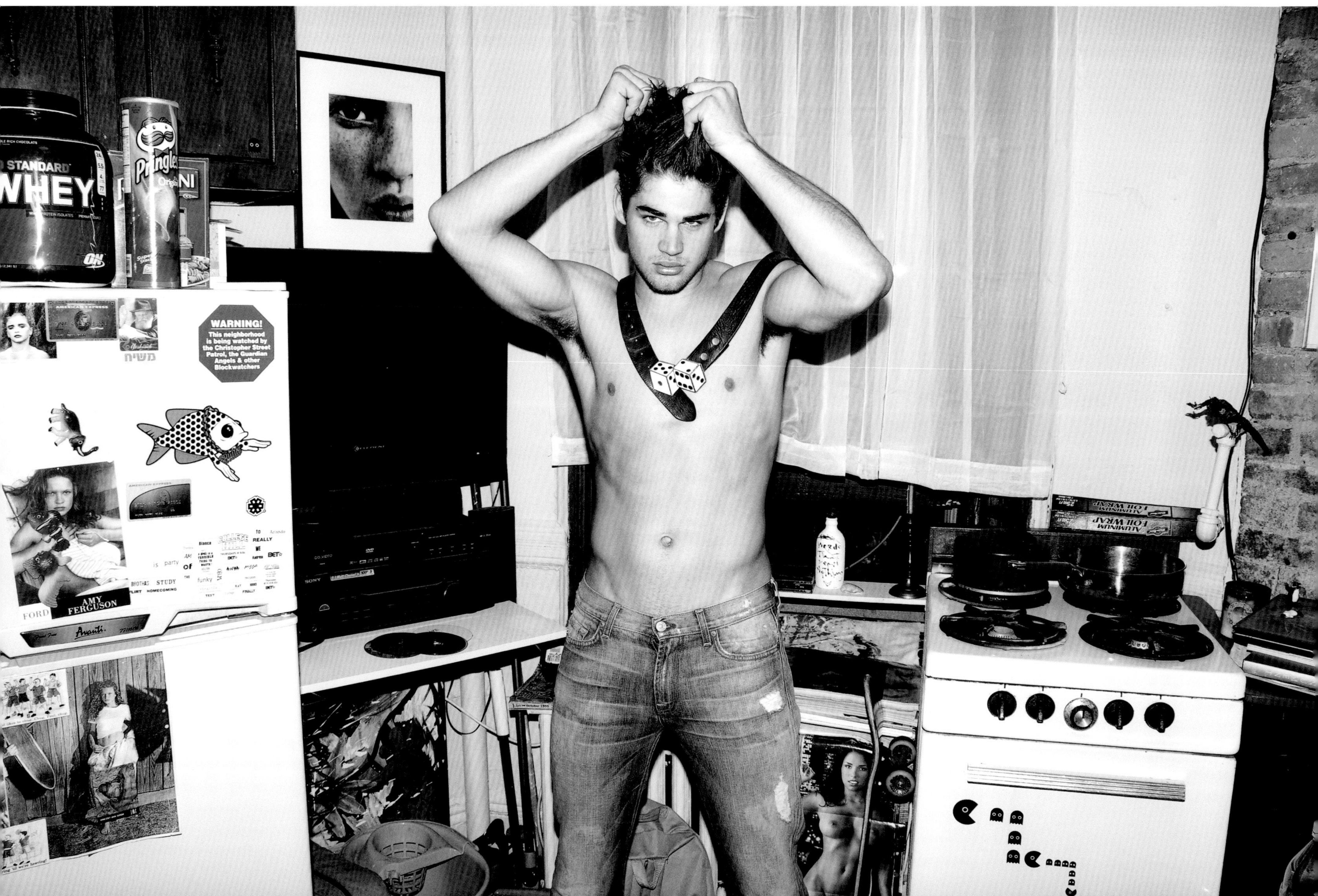

Christopher Street, New York City

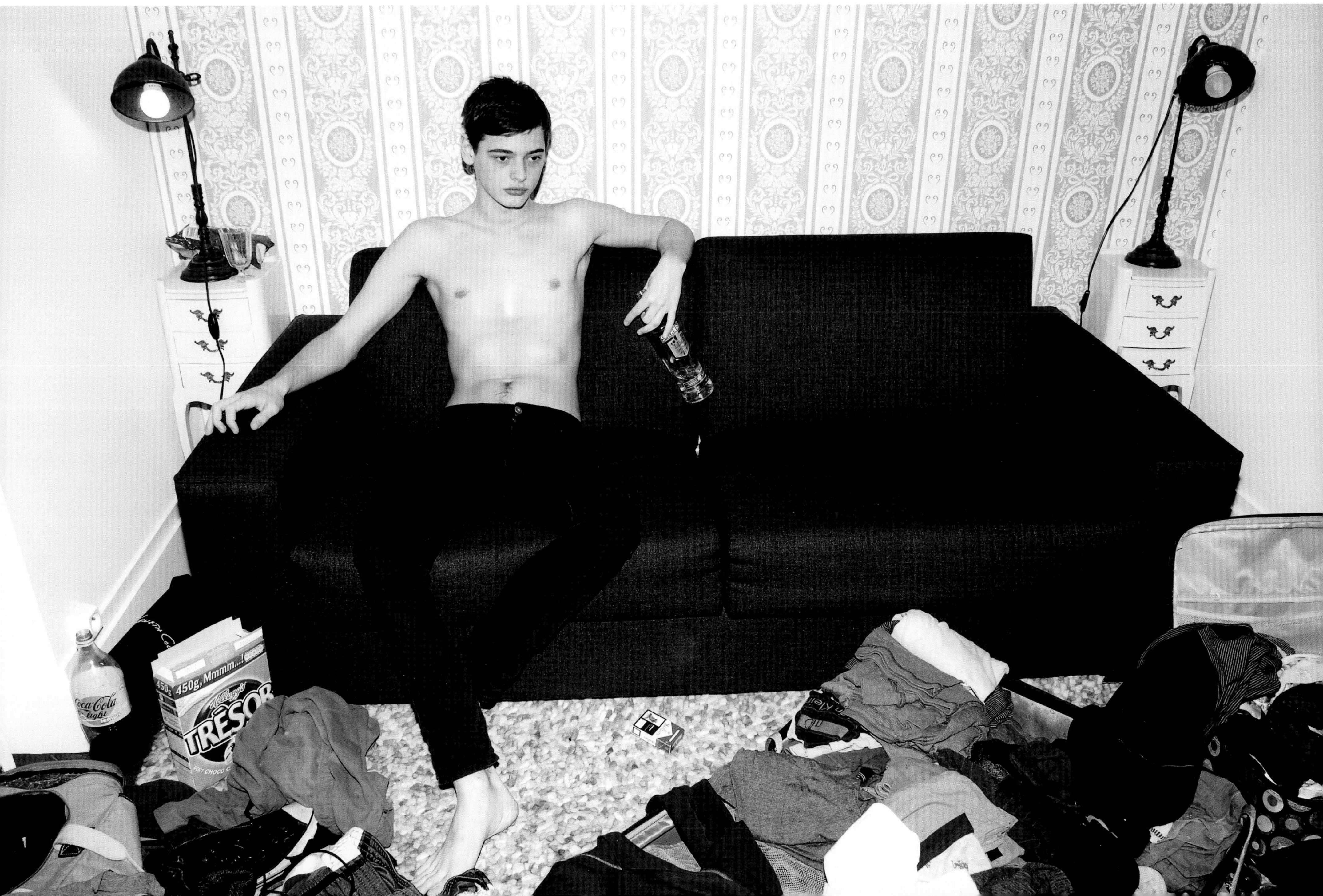

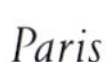

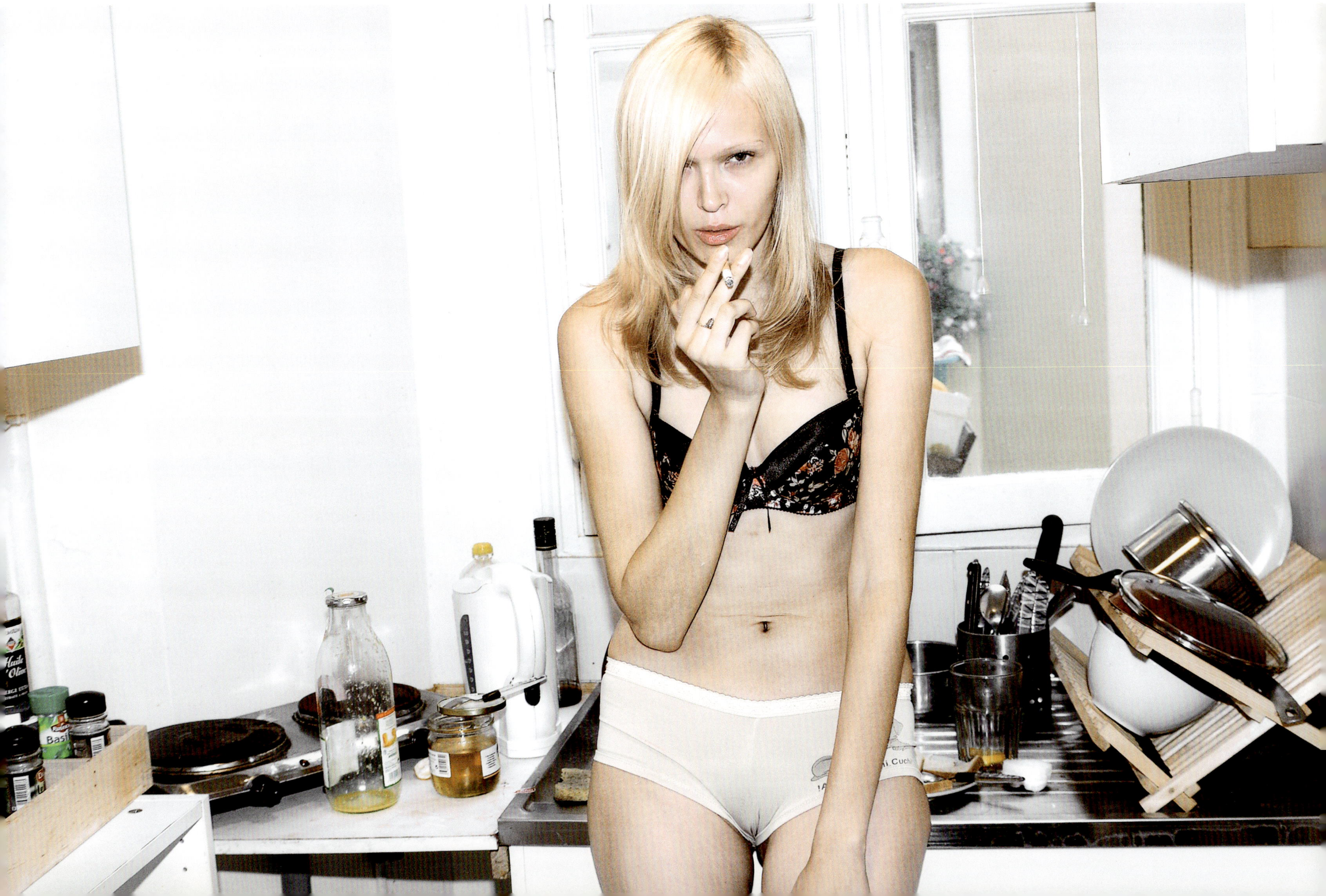

 Model apartment, 2012
New York City

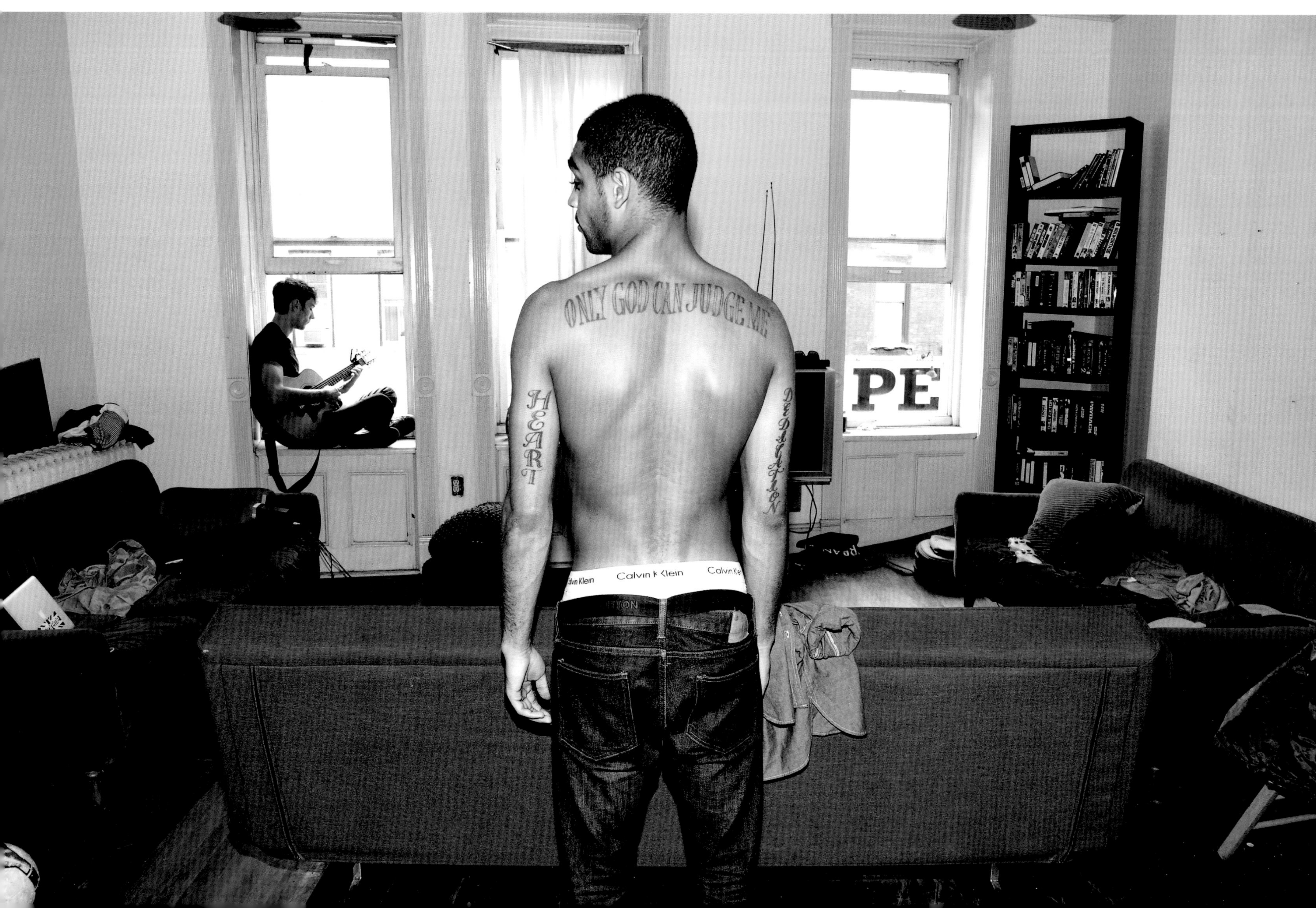

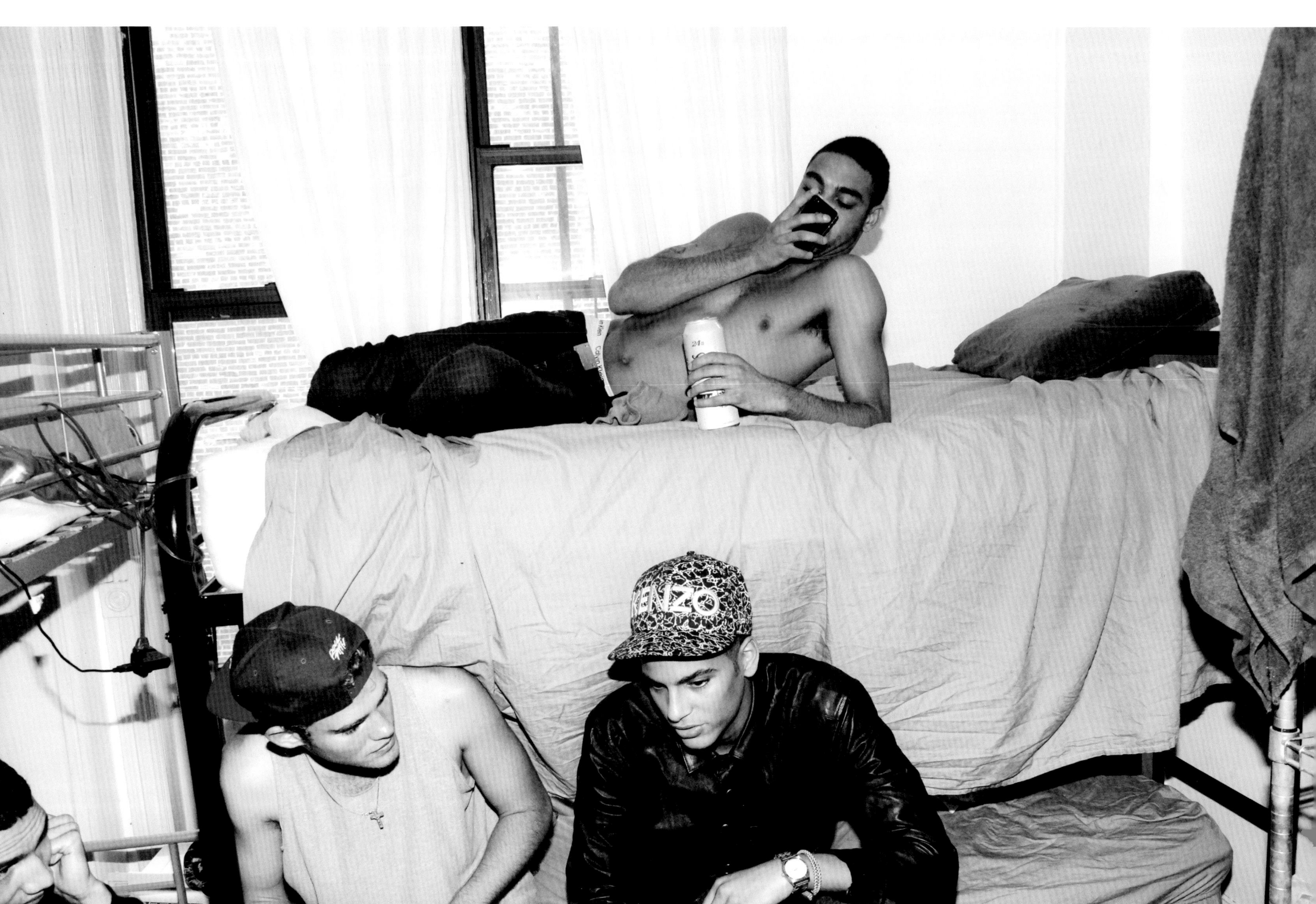

KENZO

Model apartment, 2012
New York City

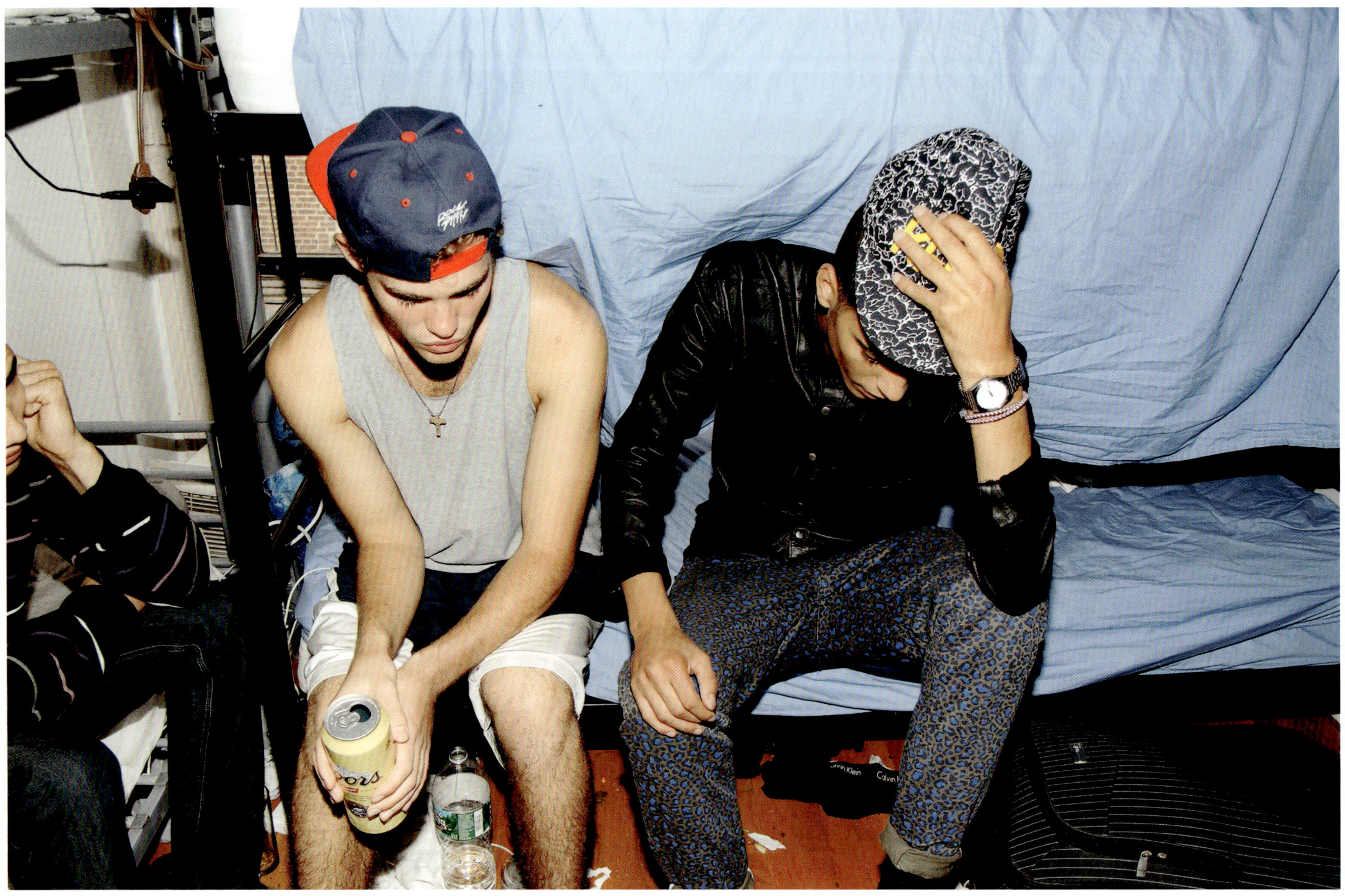

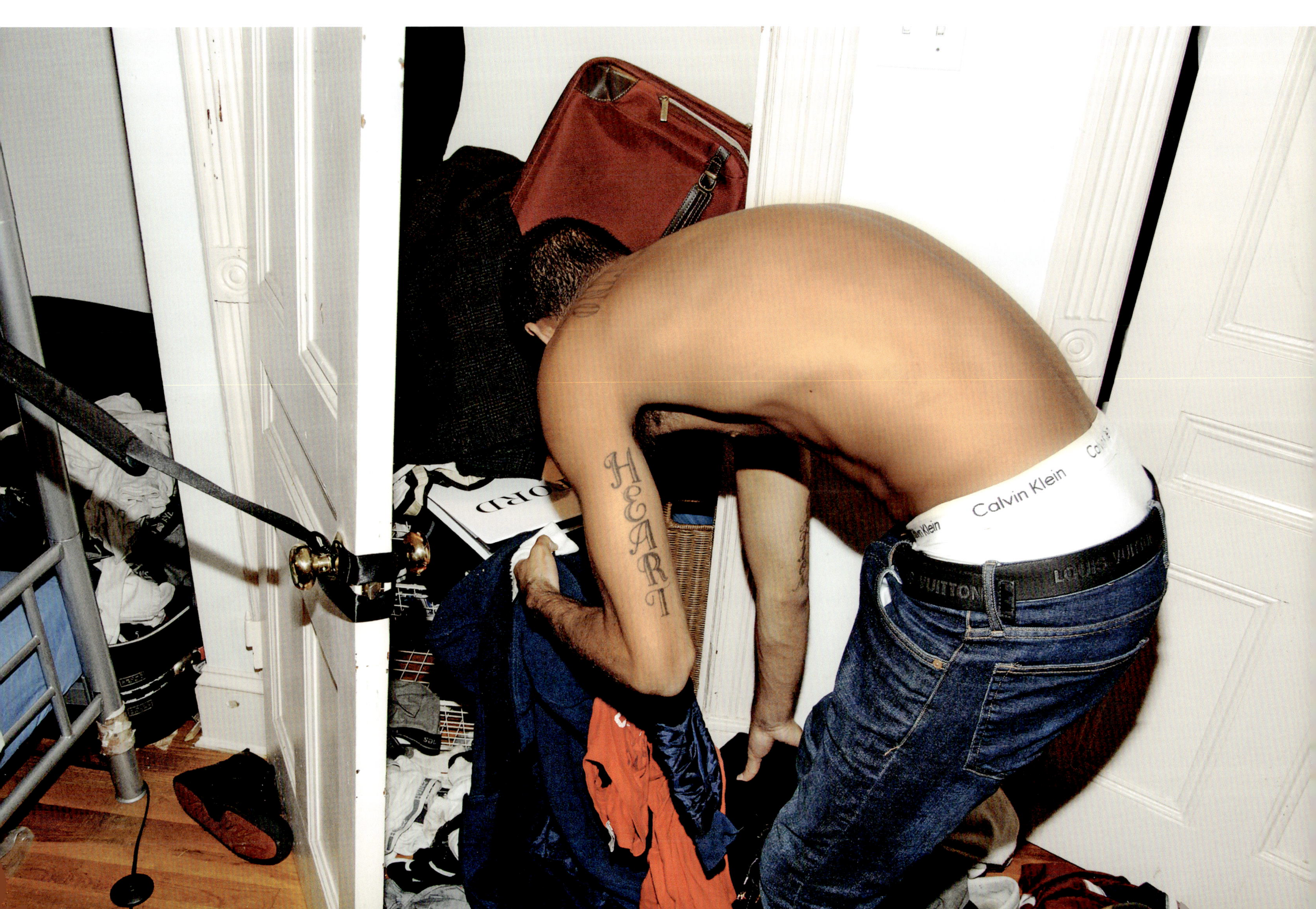

Giedre, 2013
Wall Street, New York City

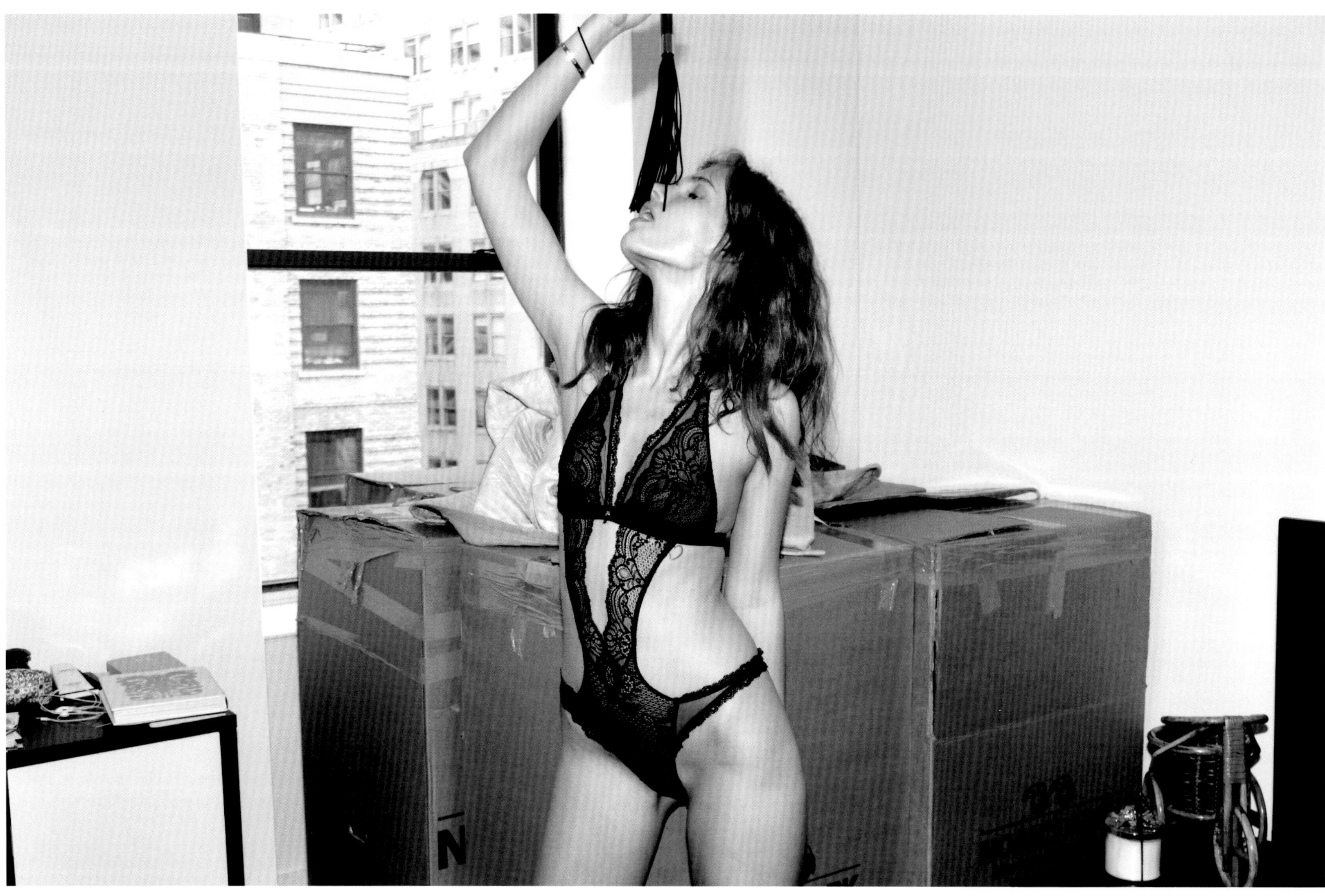

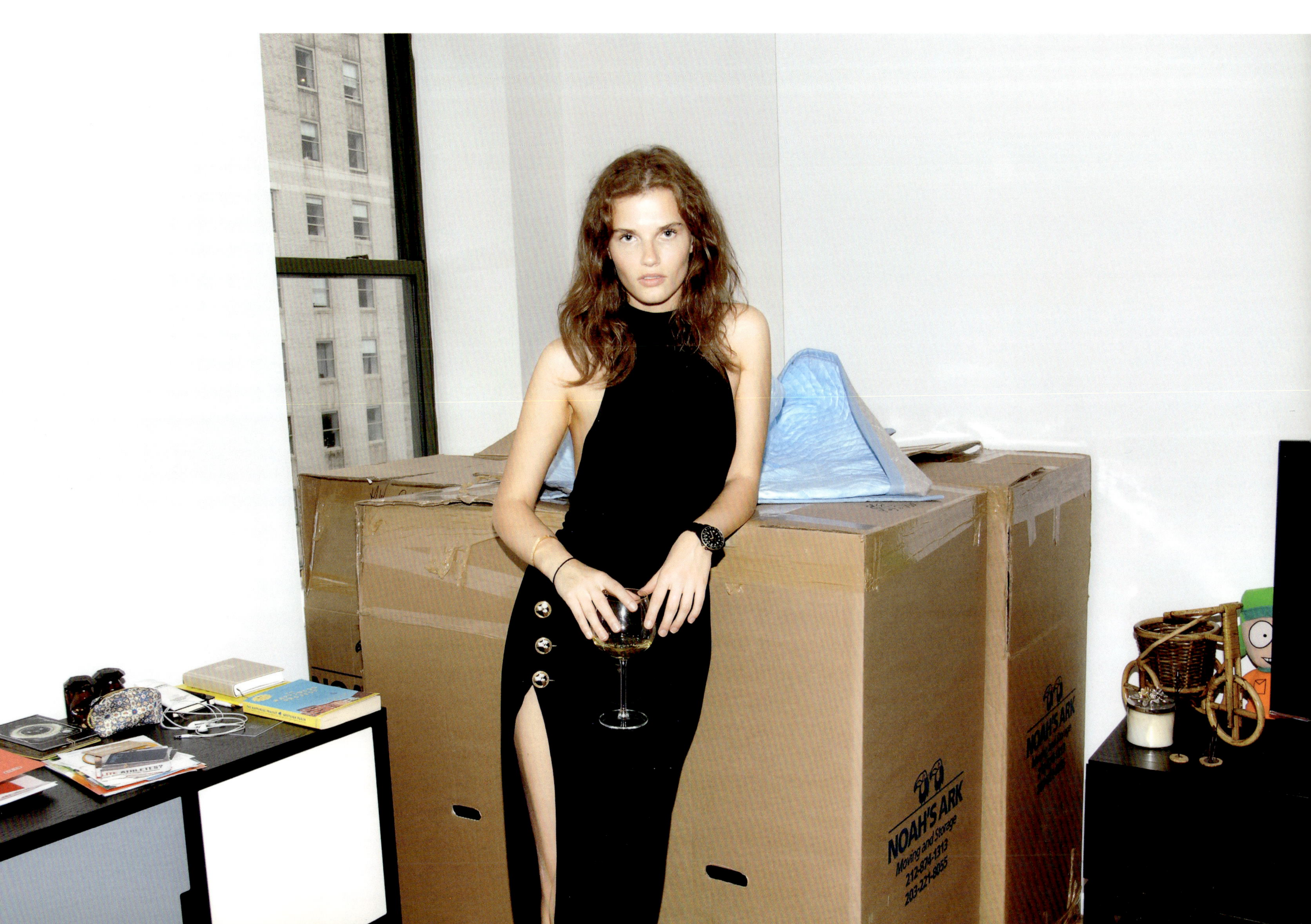

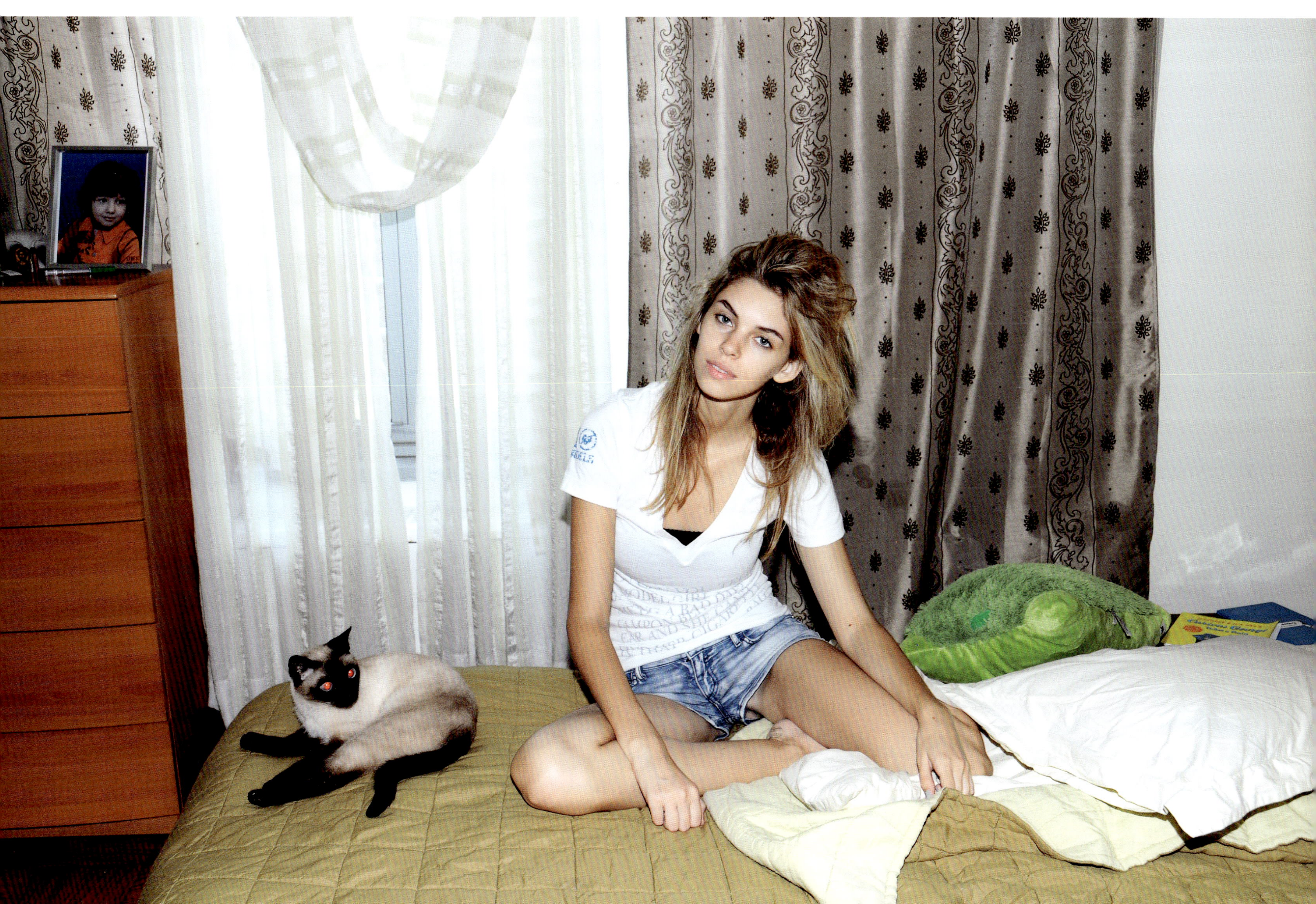

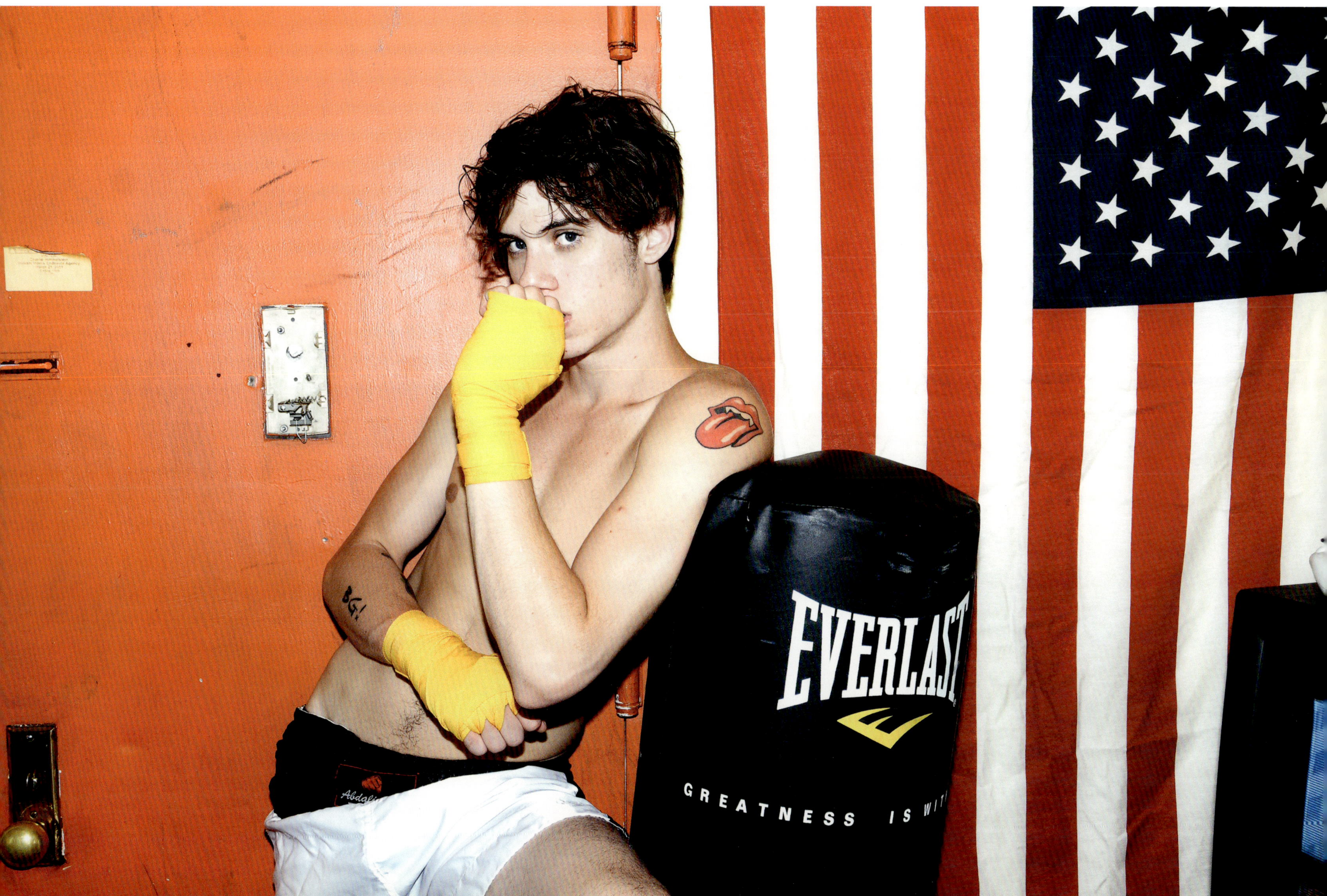
EVERLAST
GREATNESS IS WIT

Charlie at his parents', 2009
Brooklyn, New York City

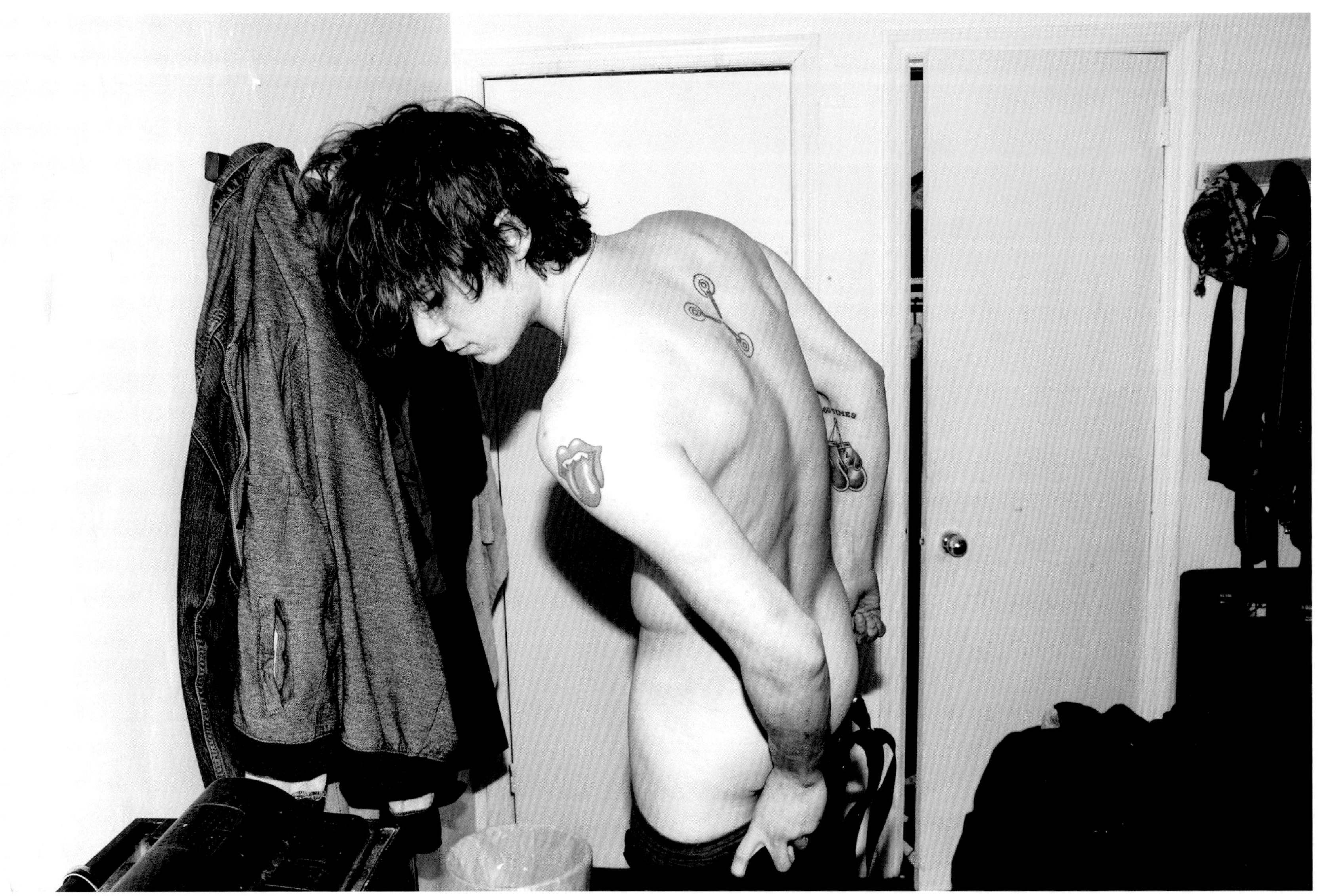

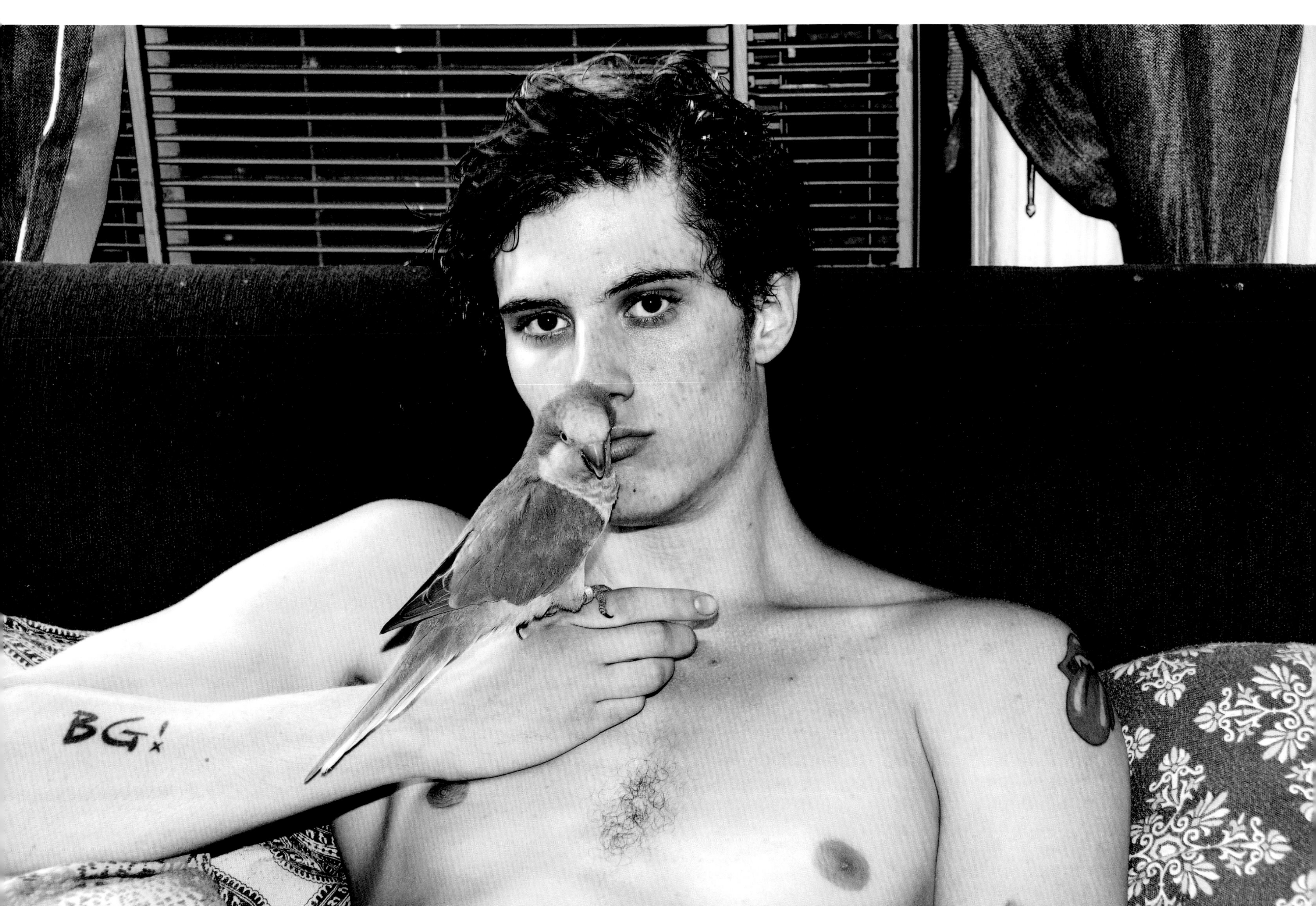
BG!
x

Brooklyn, New York City

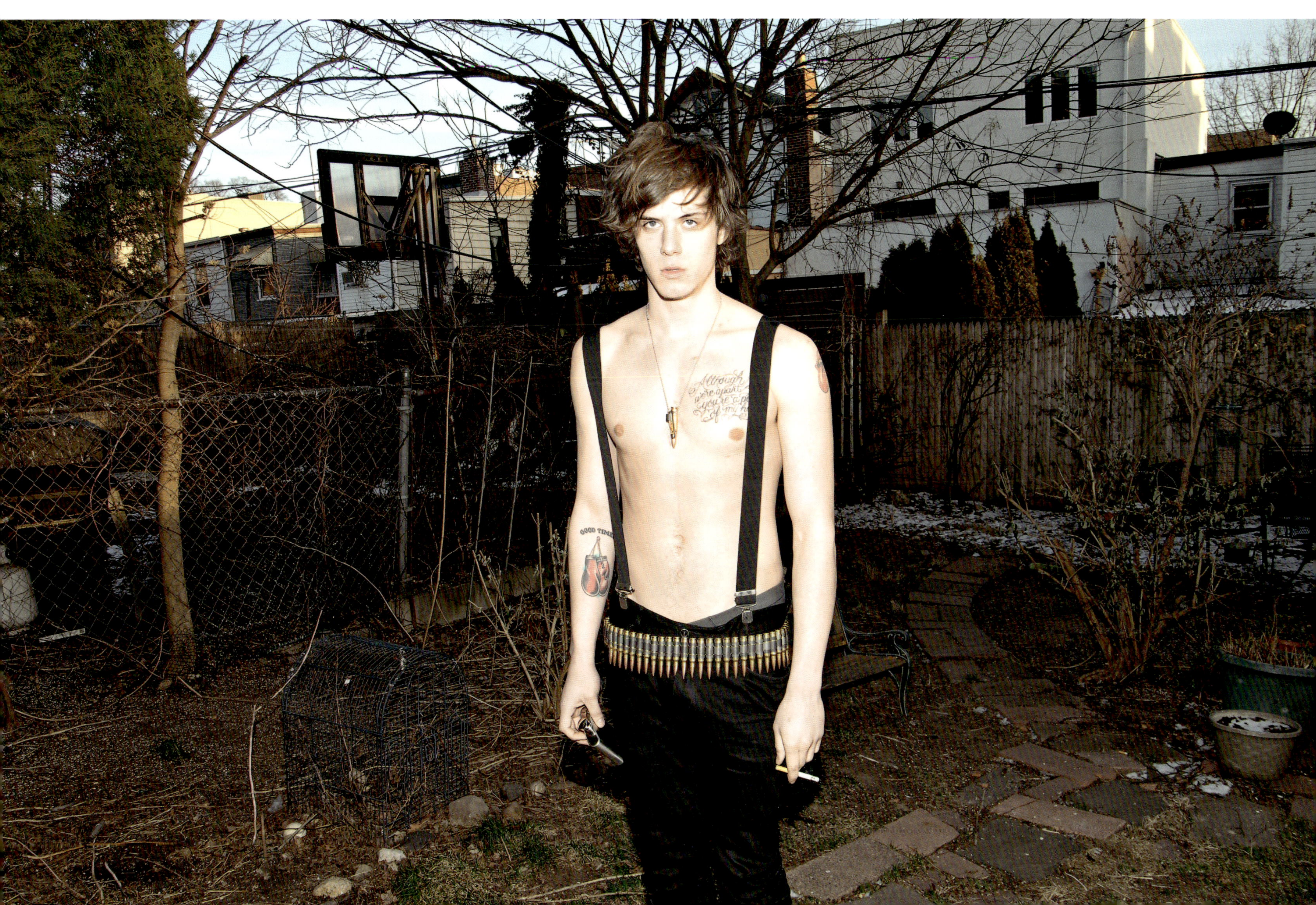

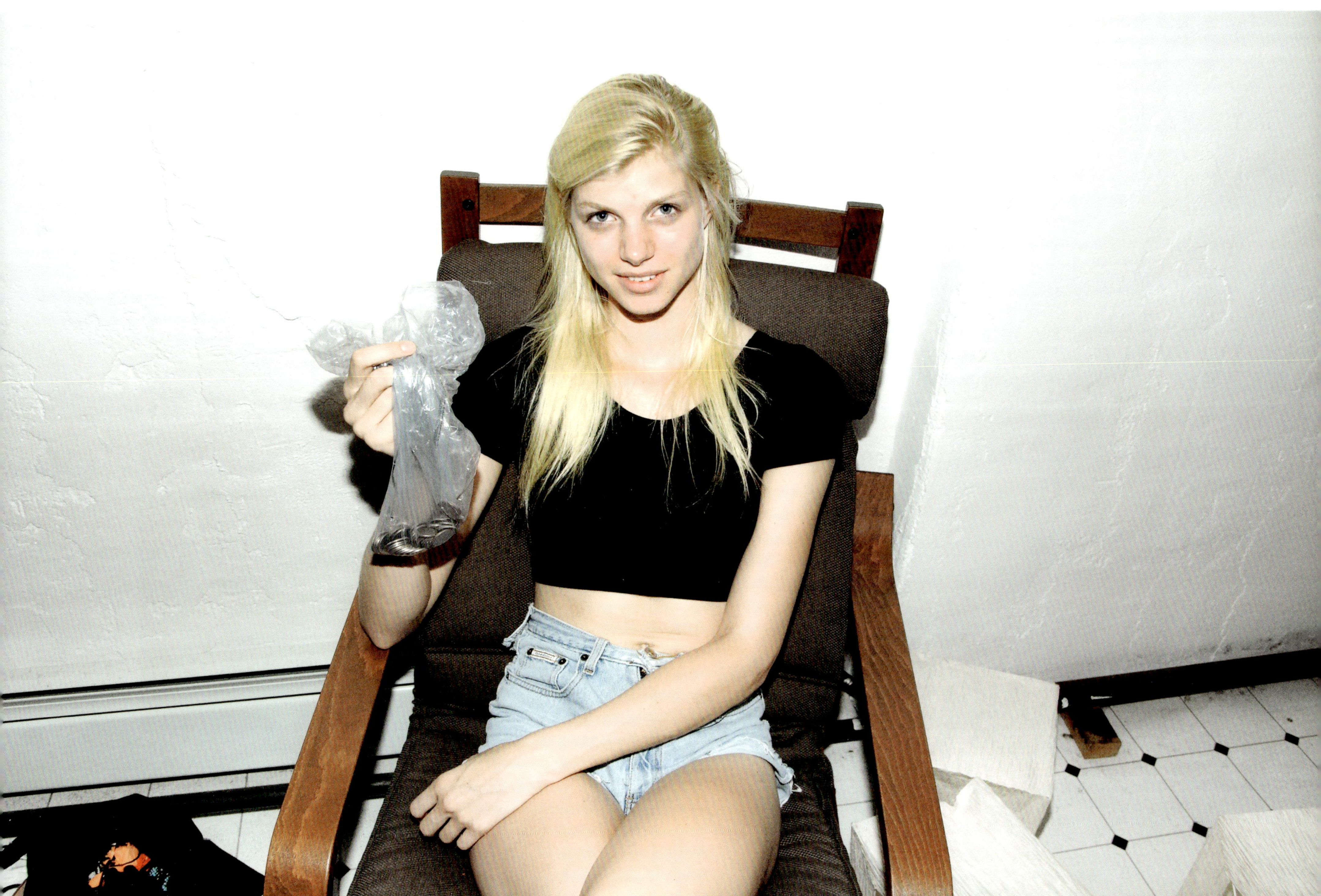

Paris

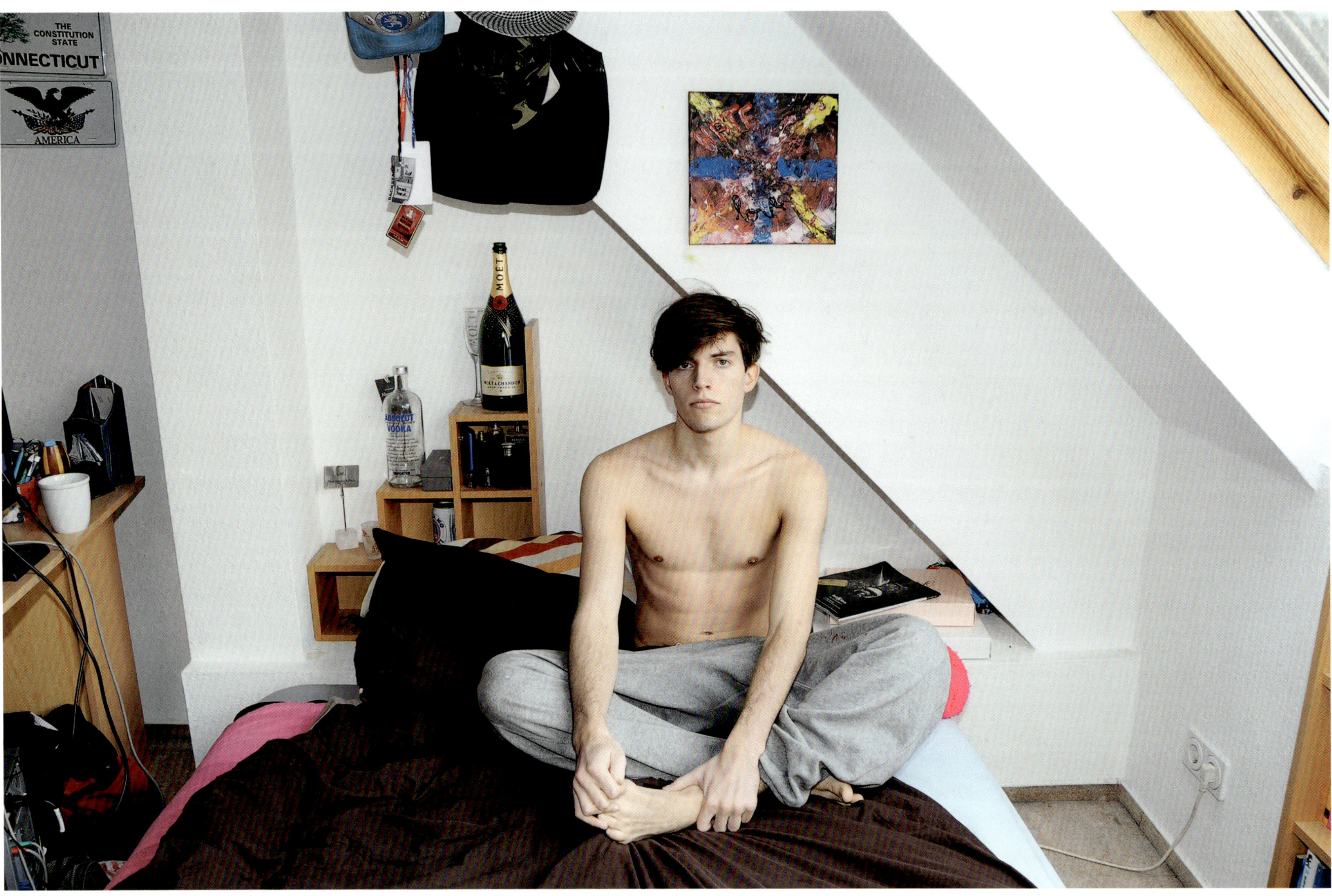

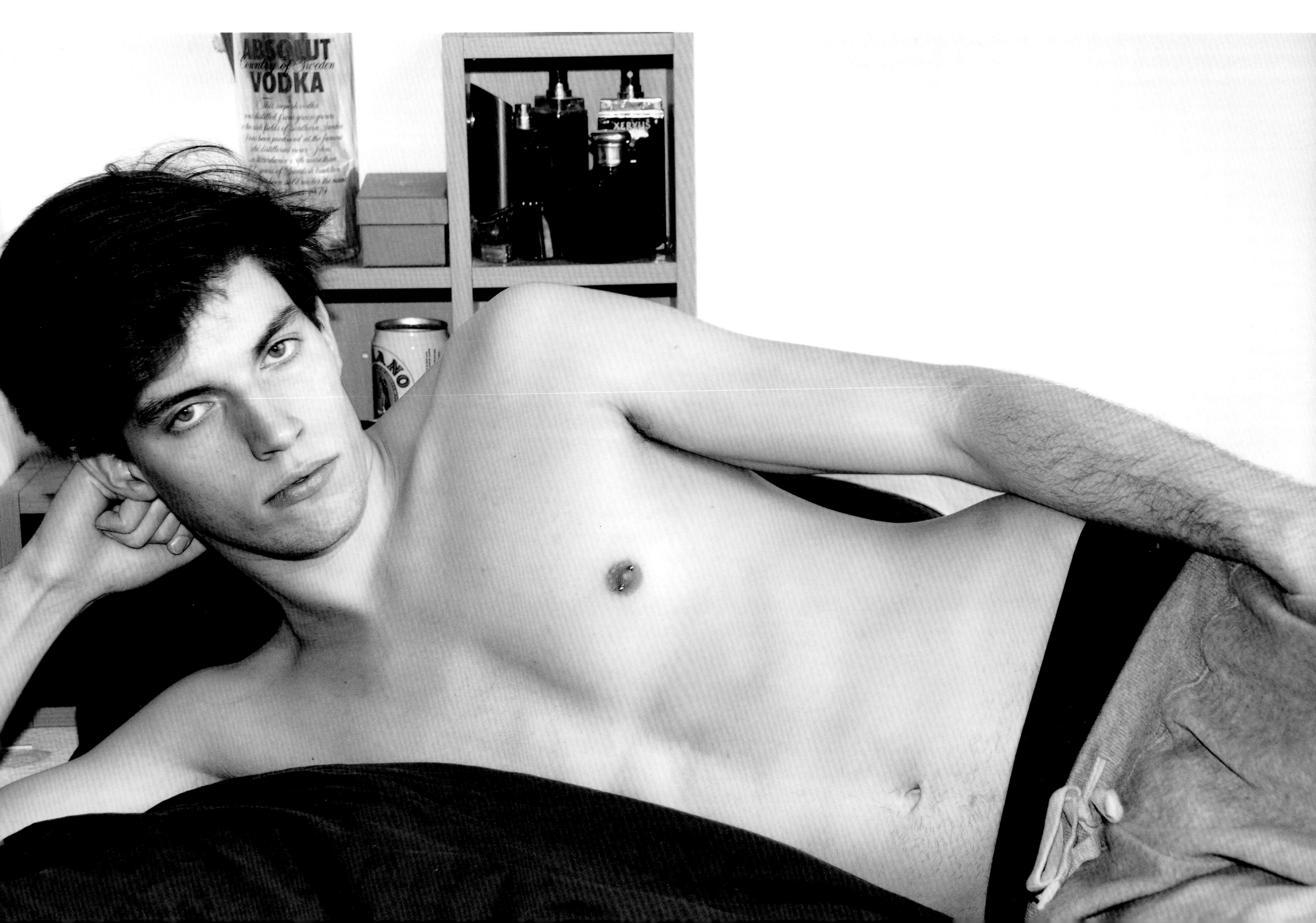
ABSOLUT
Country of Sweden
VODKA

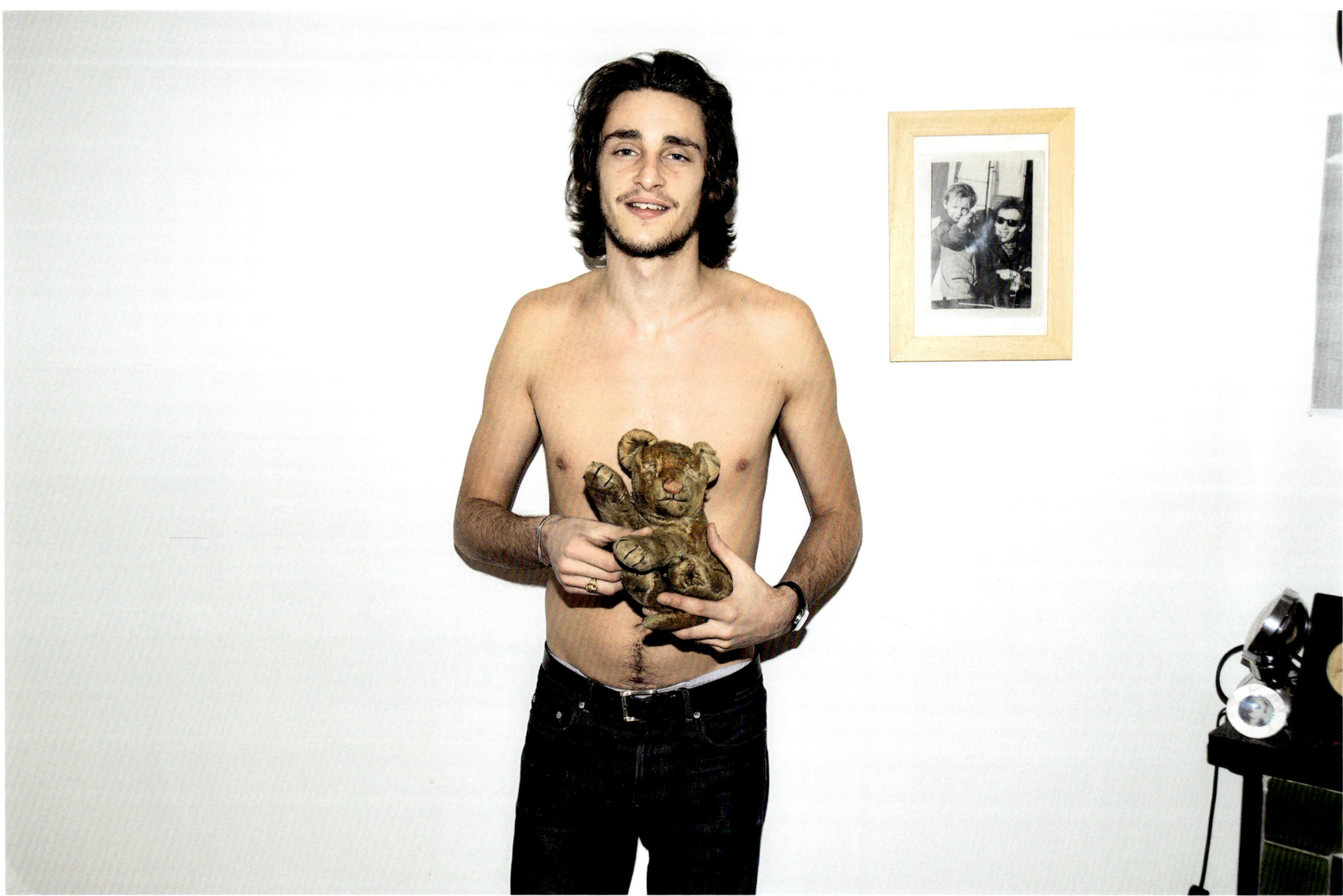

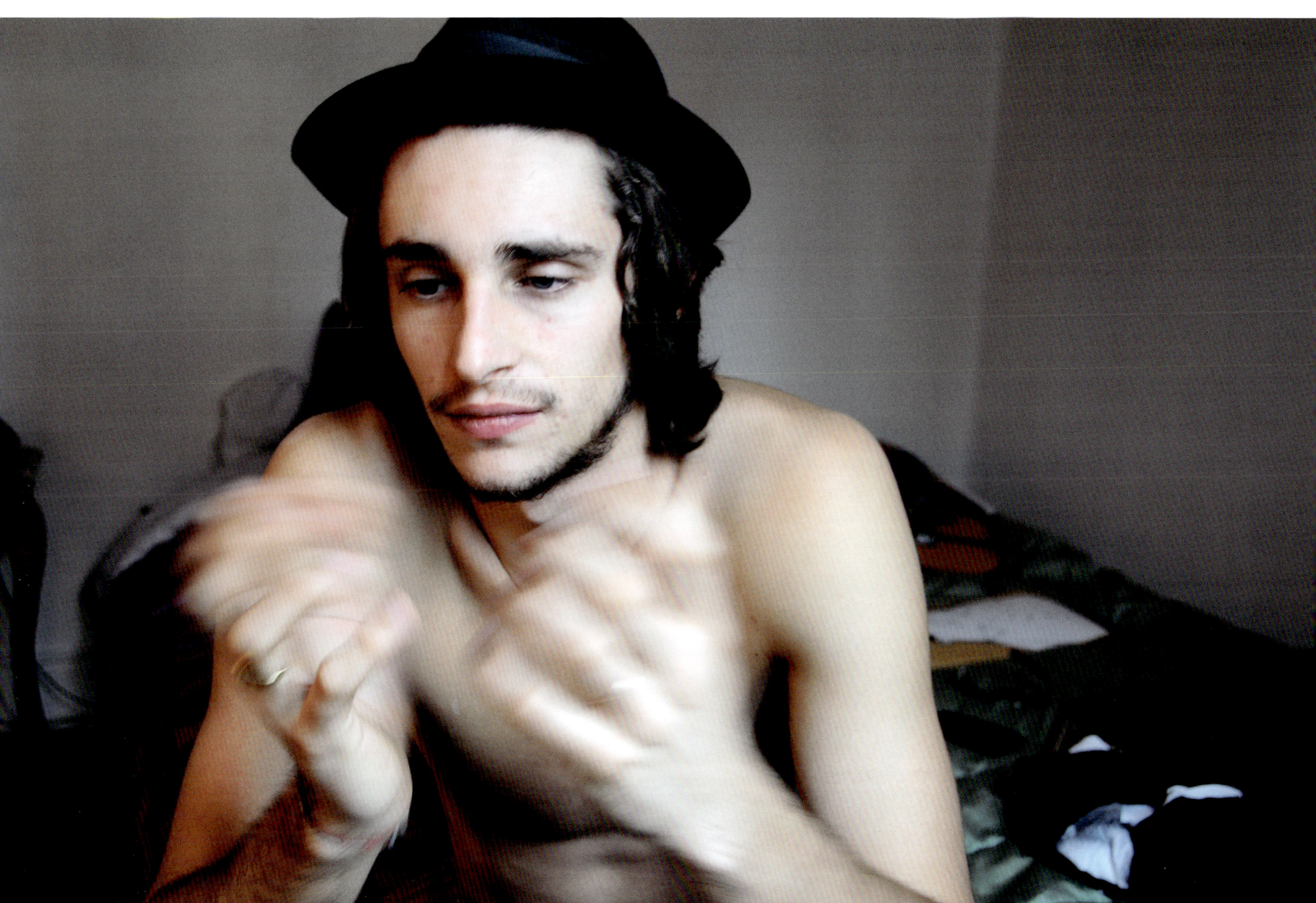

Paris

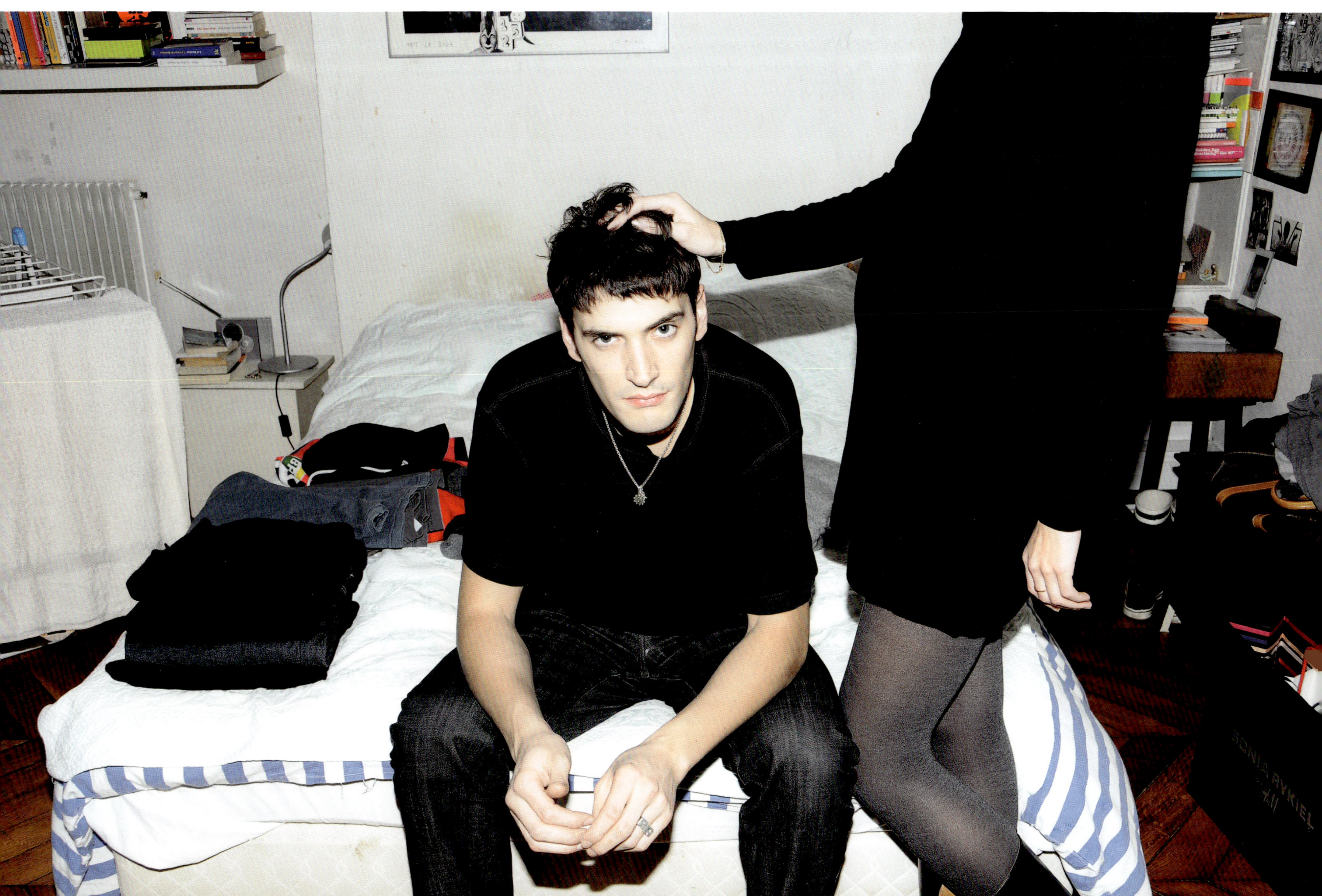

Rebecca, 2009
Paris

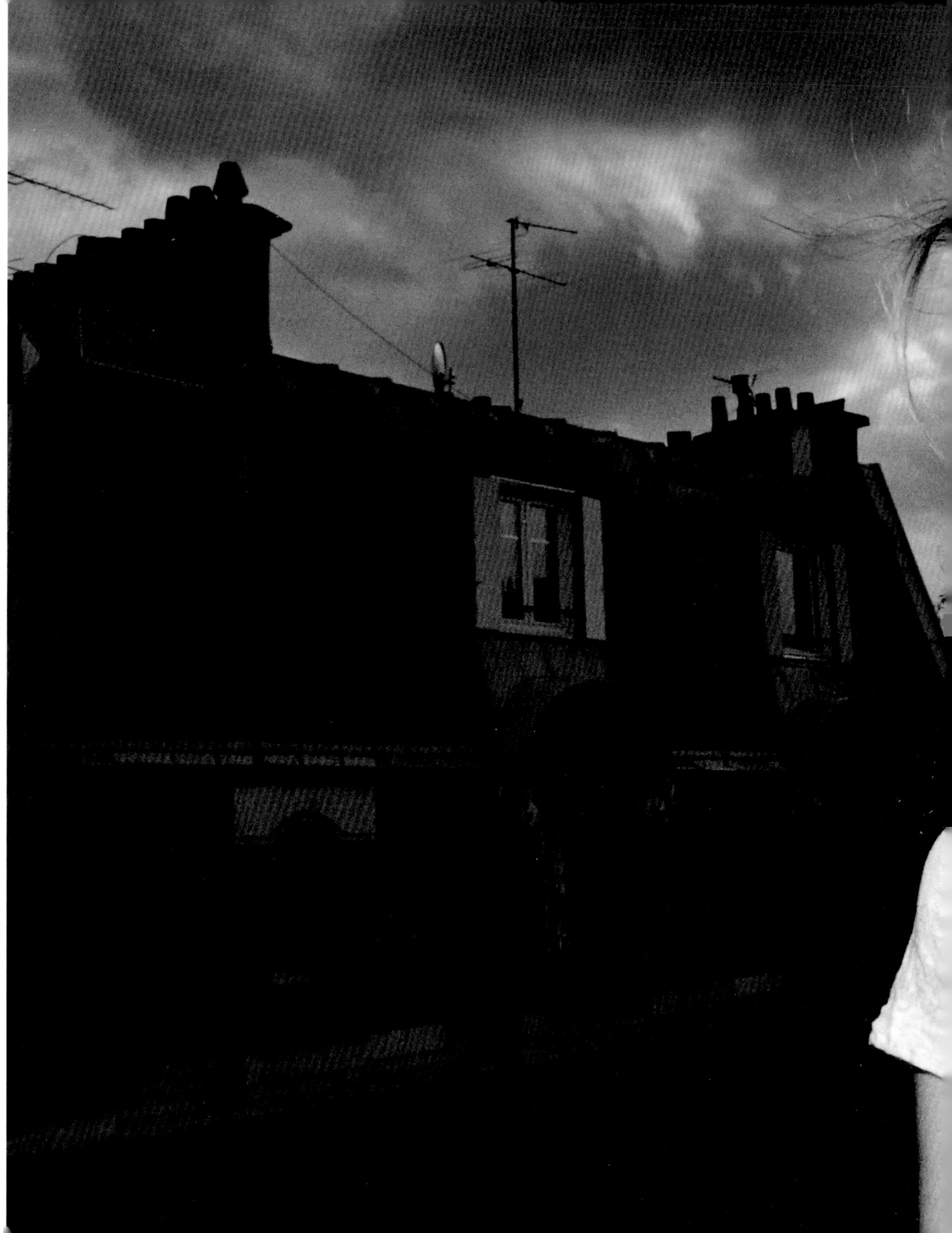

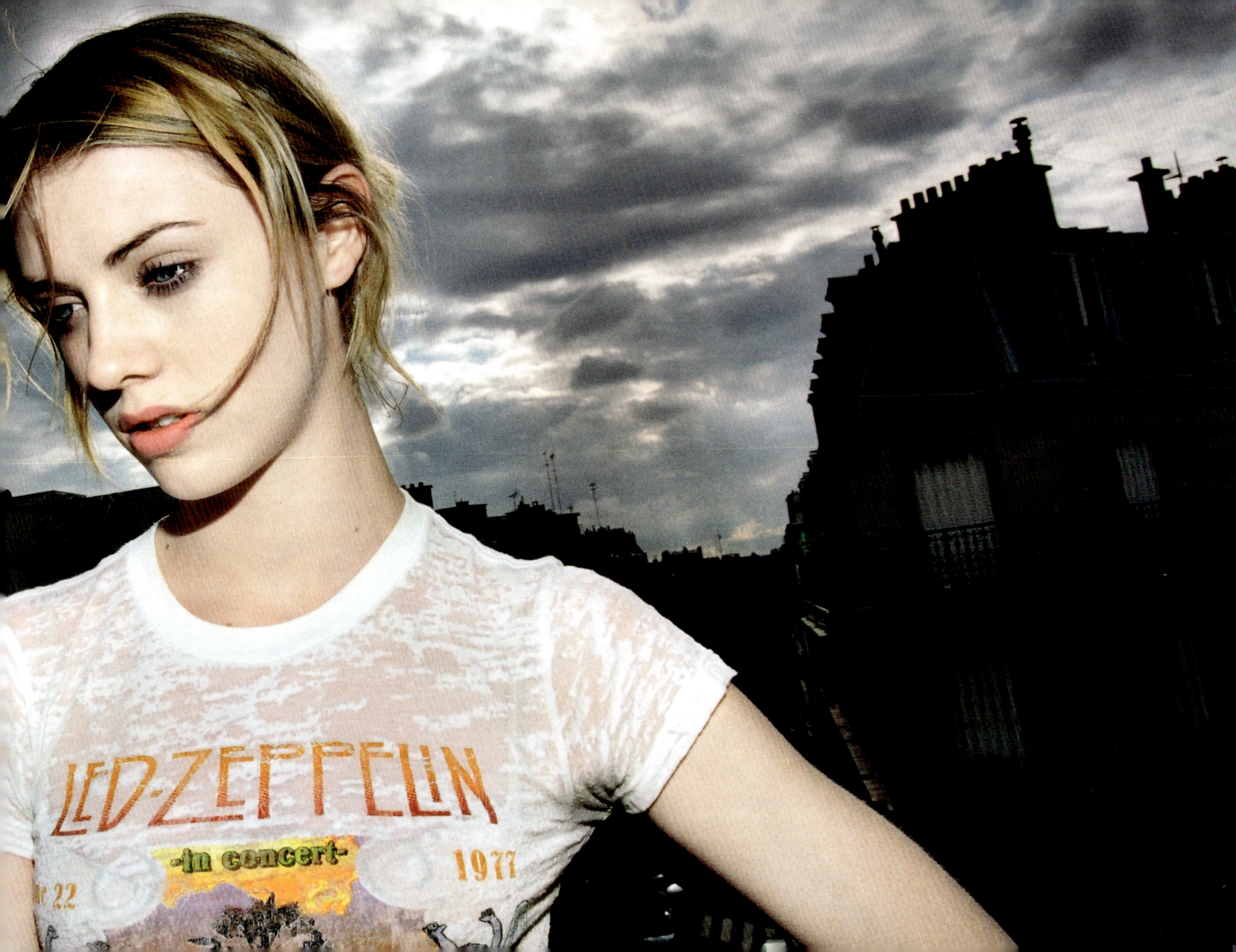
LED·ZEPPELIN
-in concert-
1977
ne 22

    Conor, model apartment, 2012
Bushwick, New York City

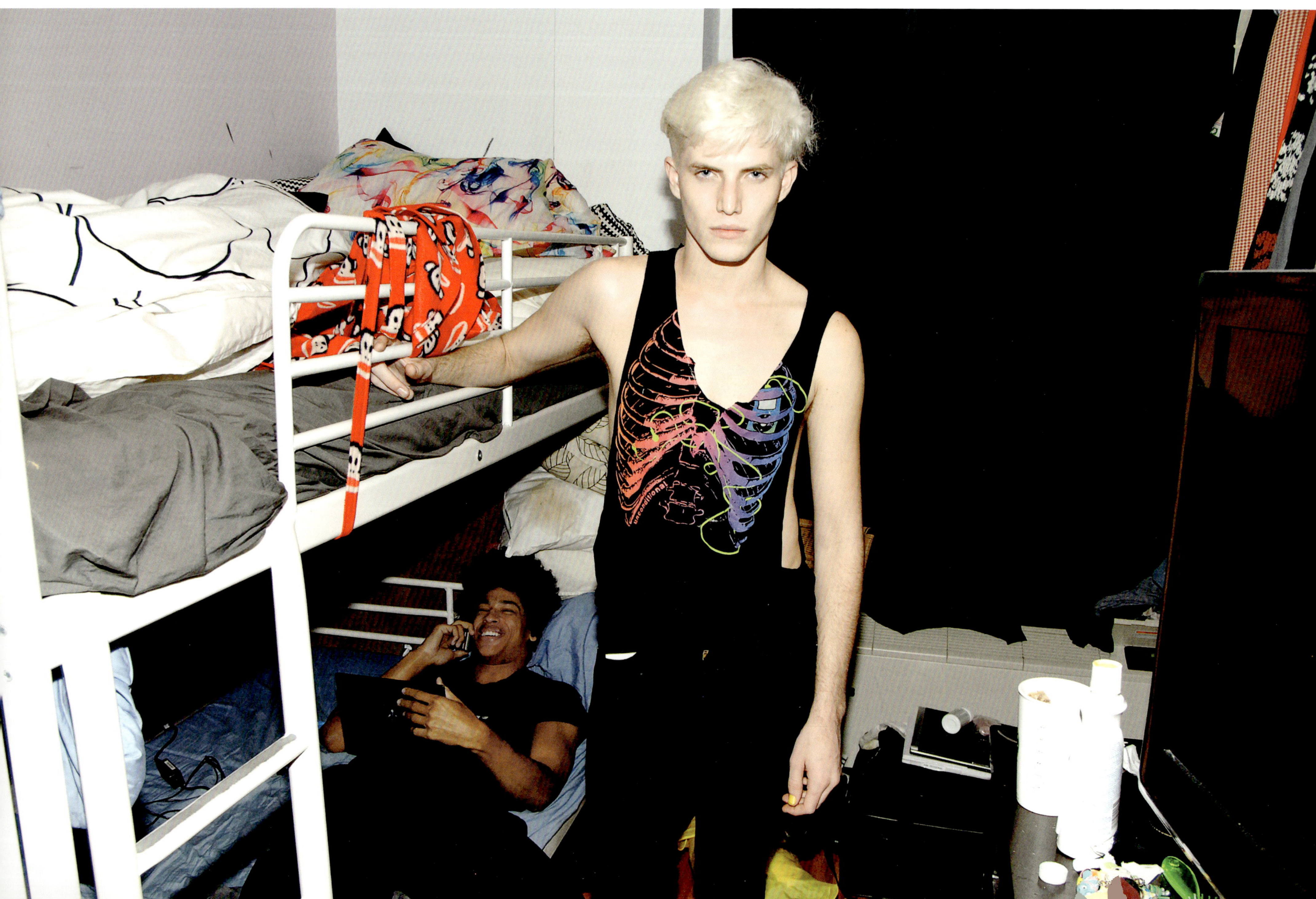

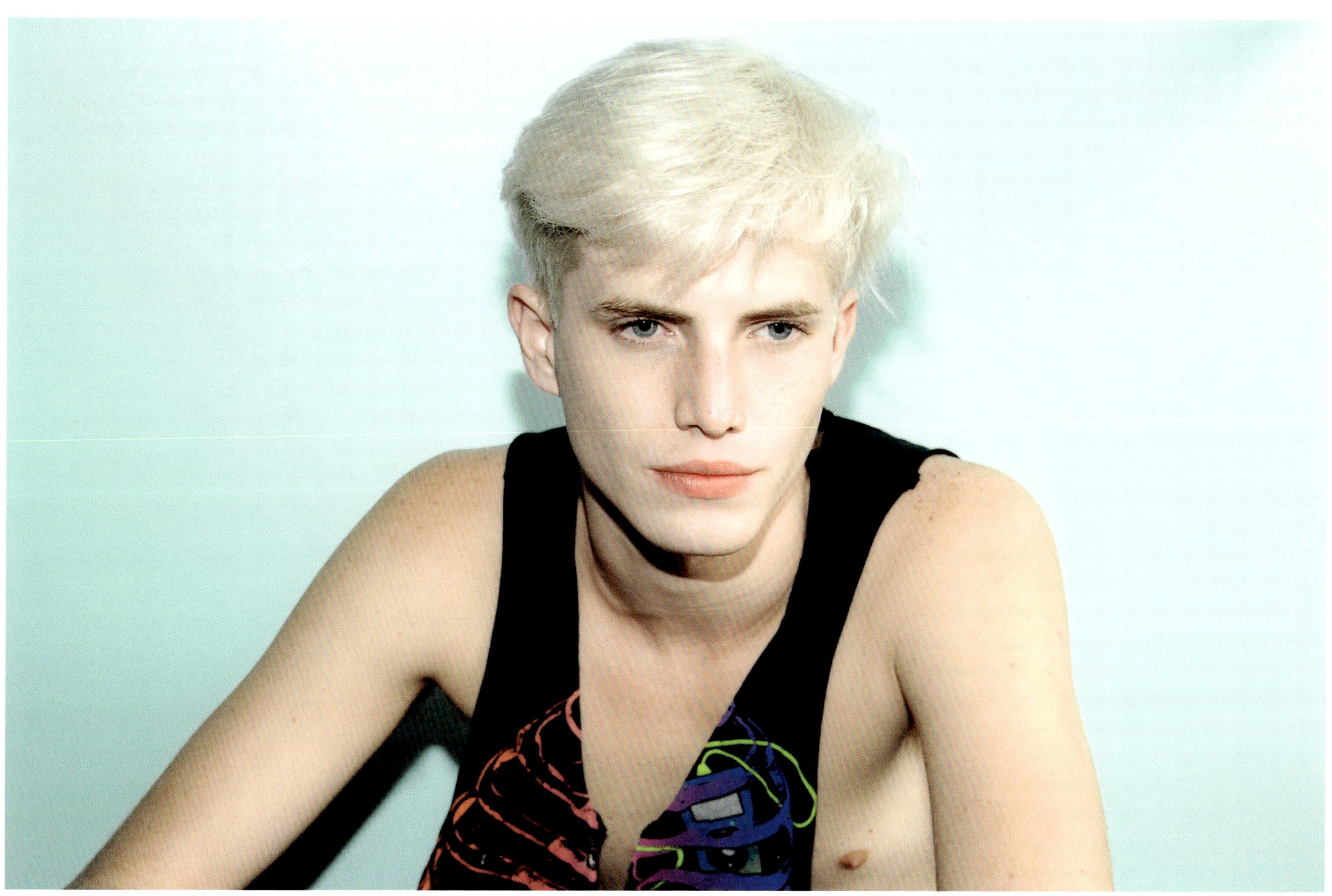

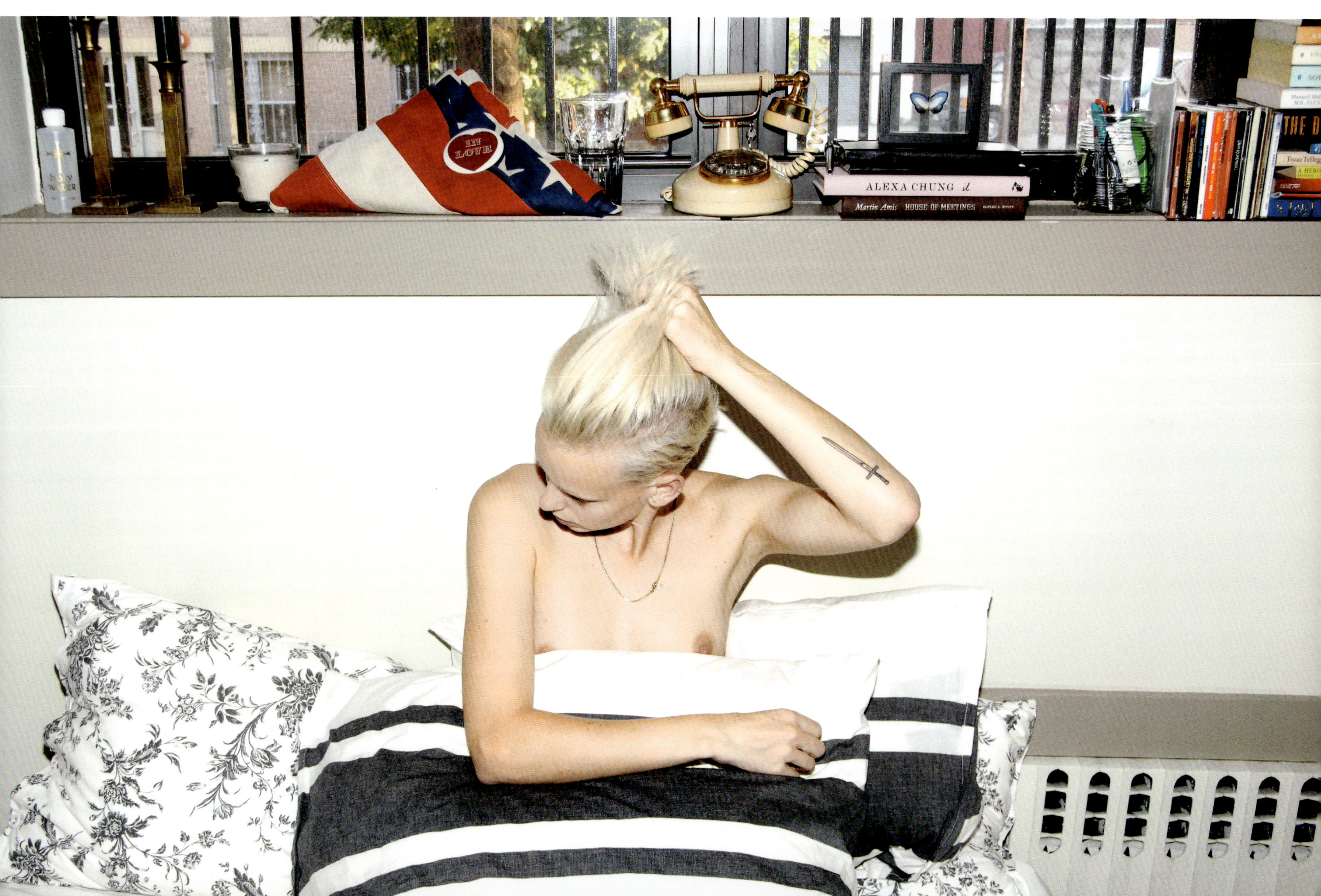

Alexey, 2013
The Bronx, New York City

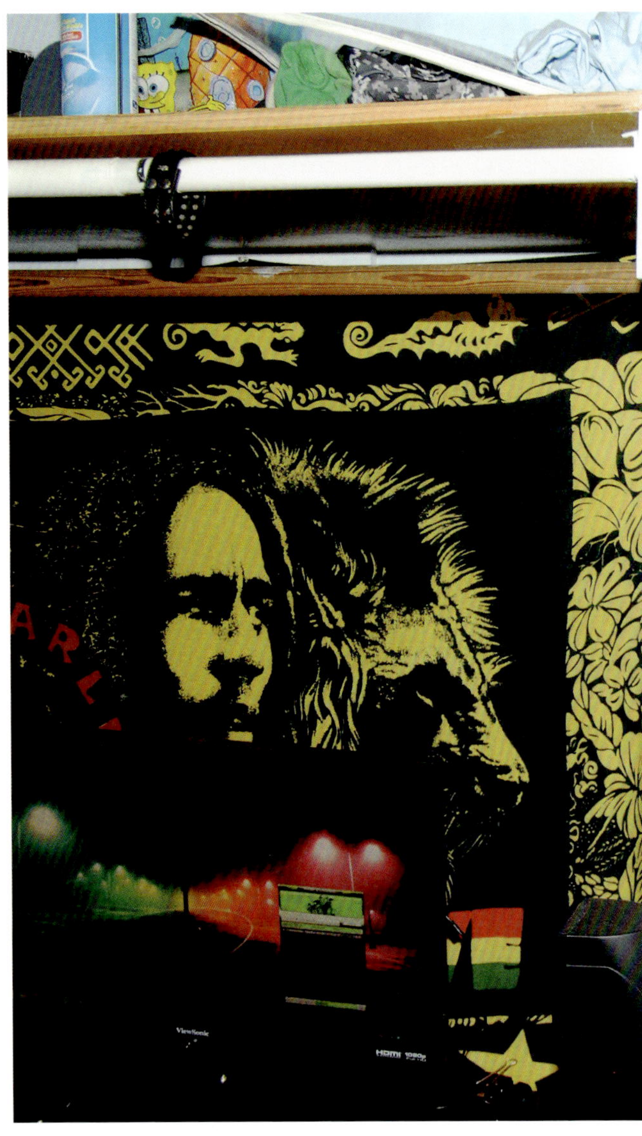

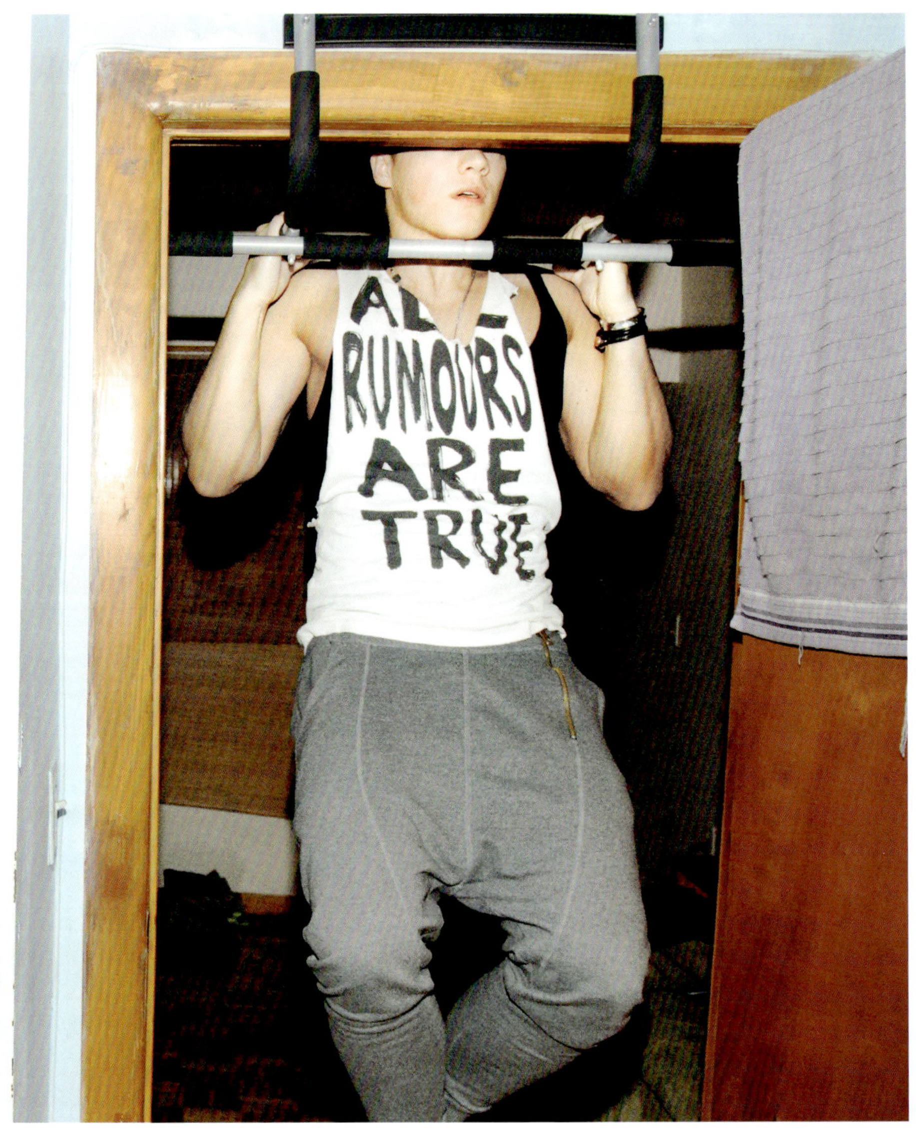

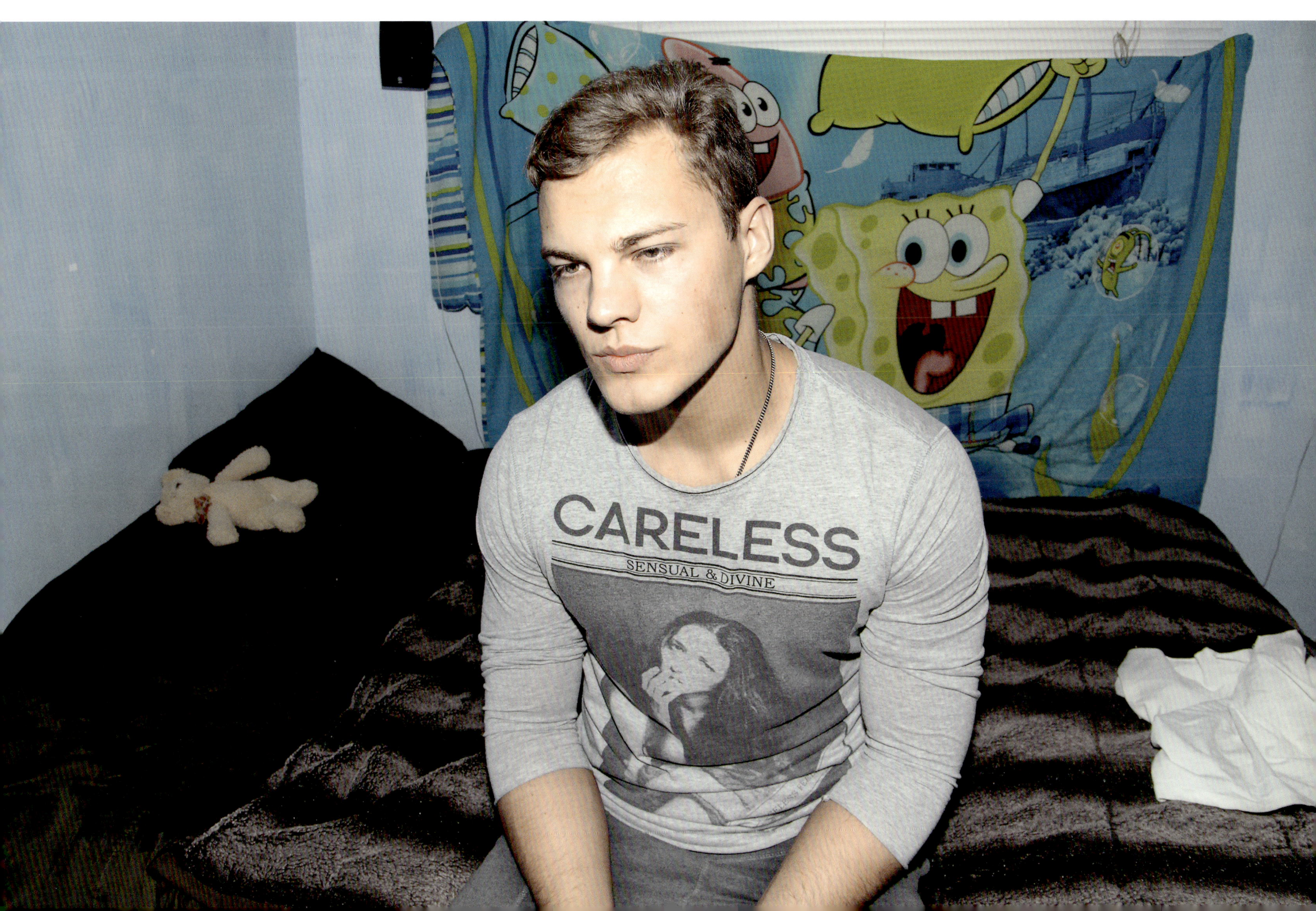

CARELESS
SENSUAL & DIVINE

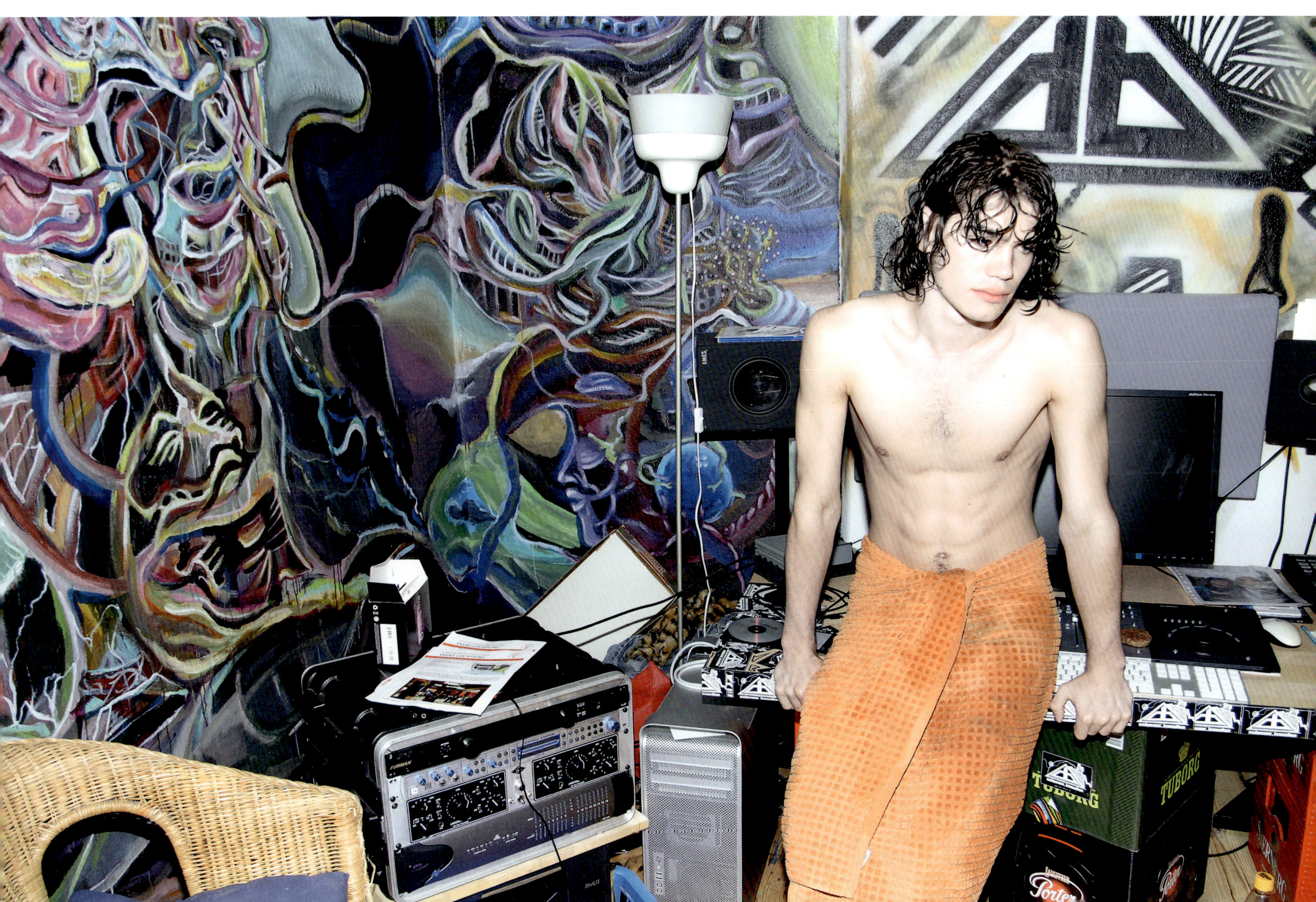

 Folka, 2015
Berlin

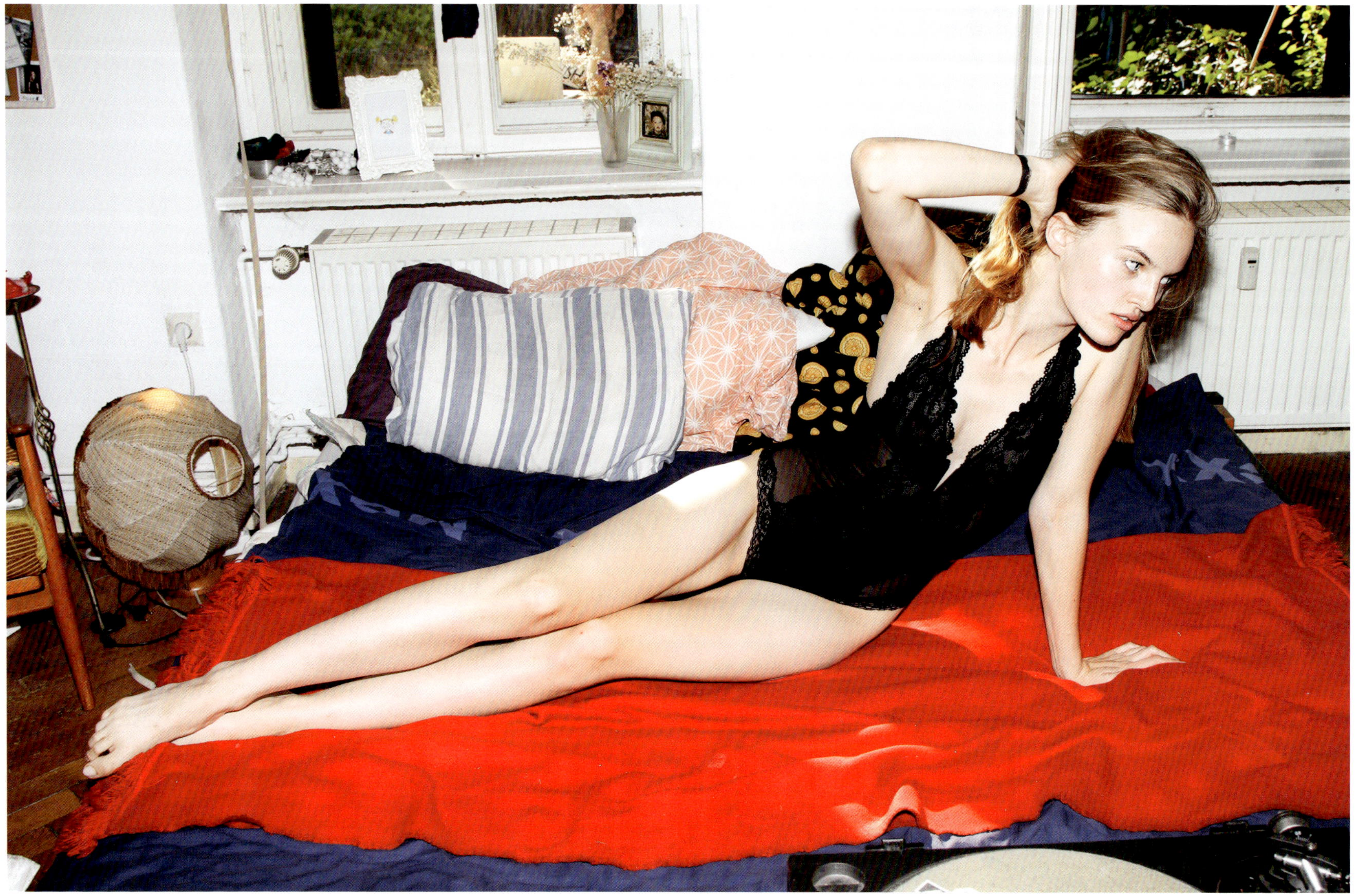

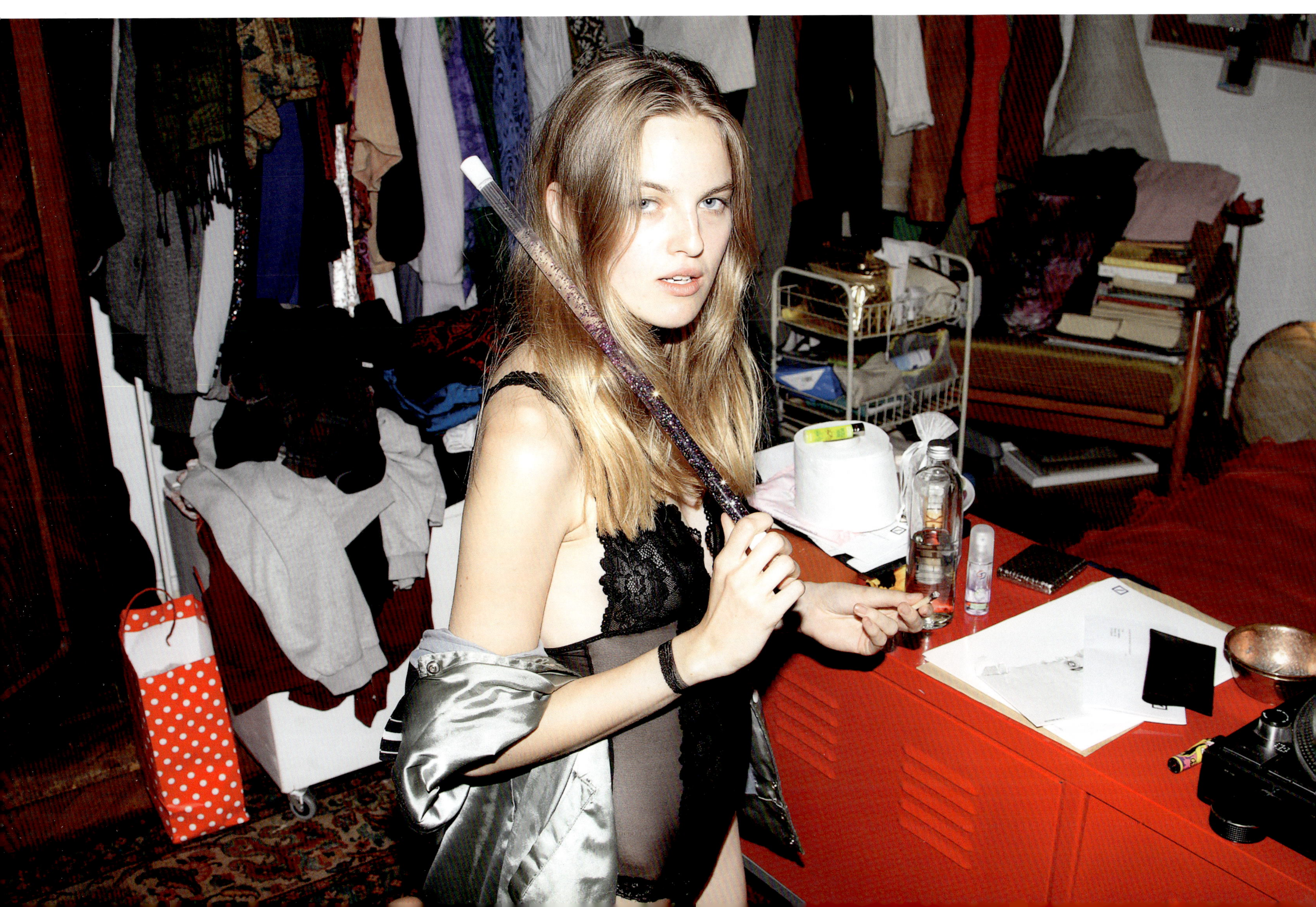

Erik at his parents', 2016
Munich

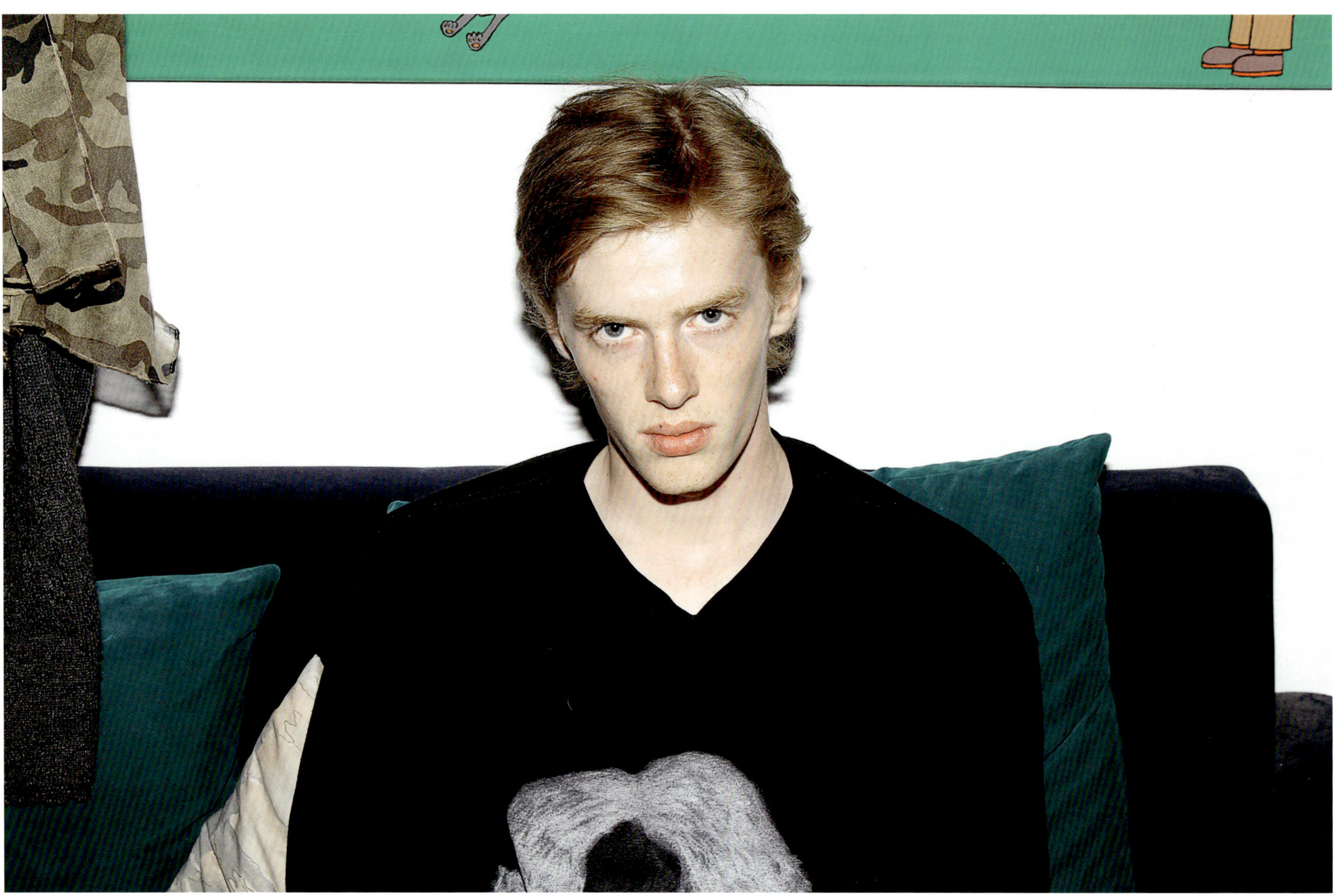

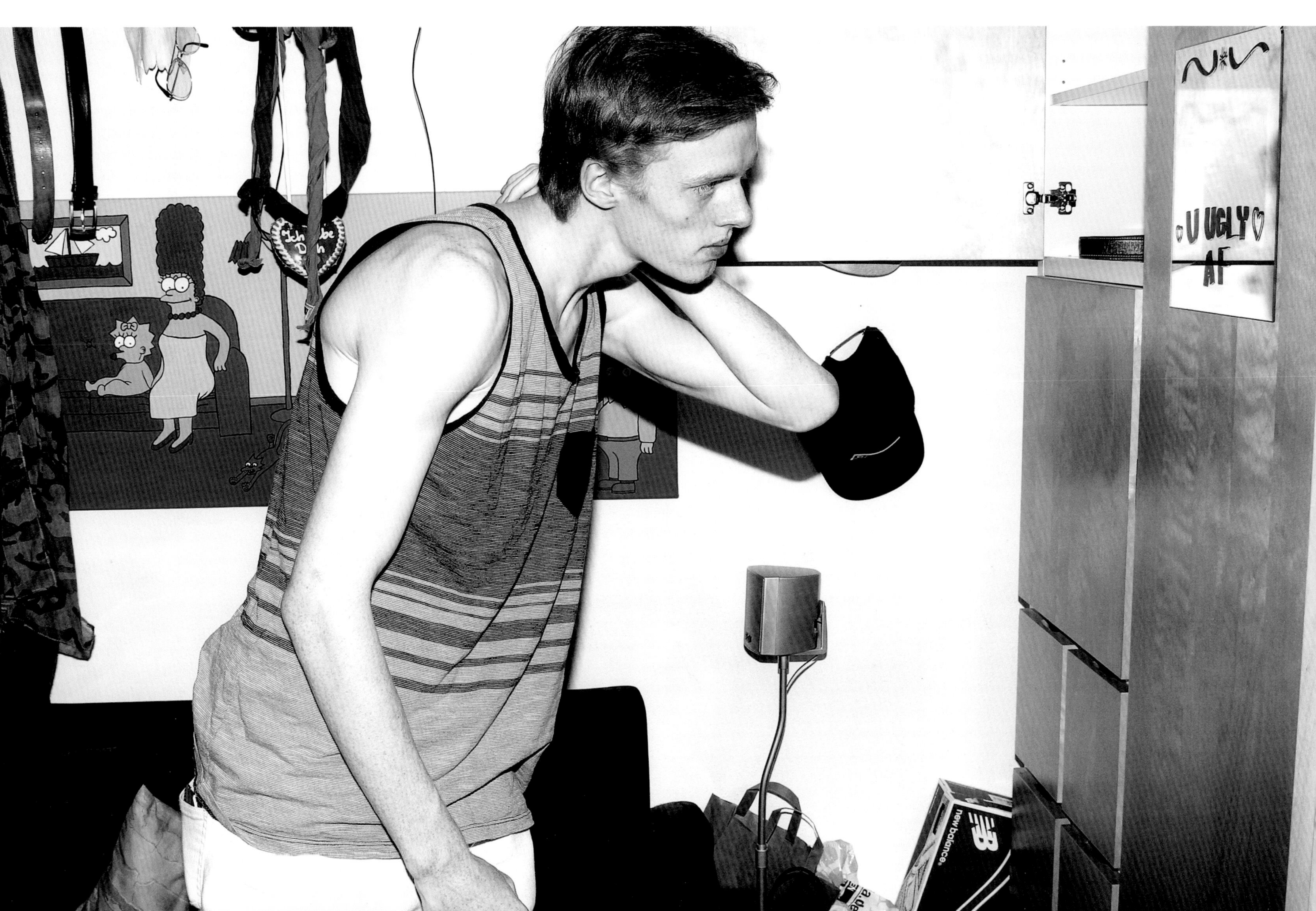
U UGLY
AF
new balance

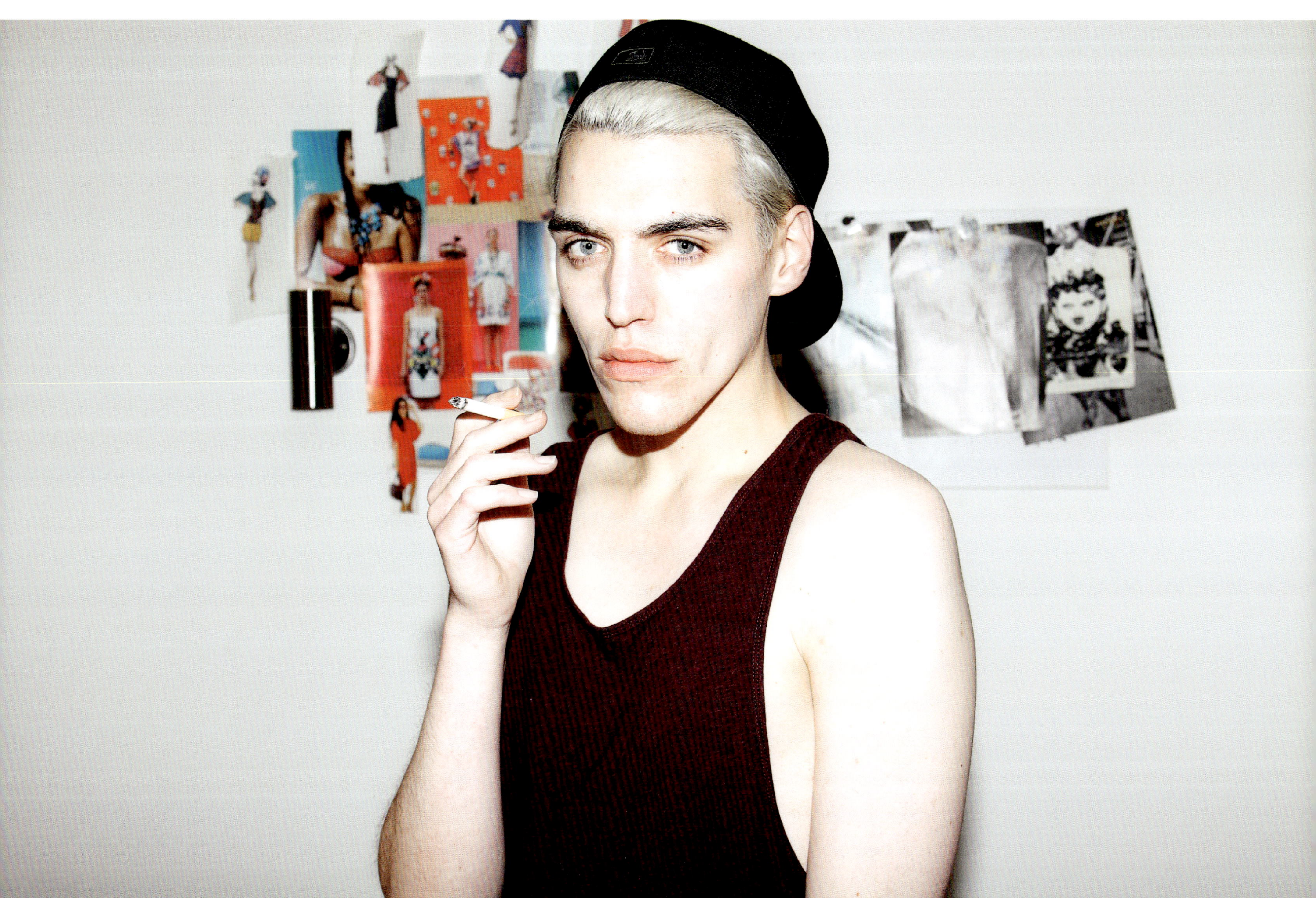

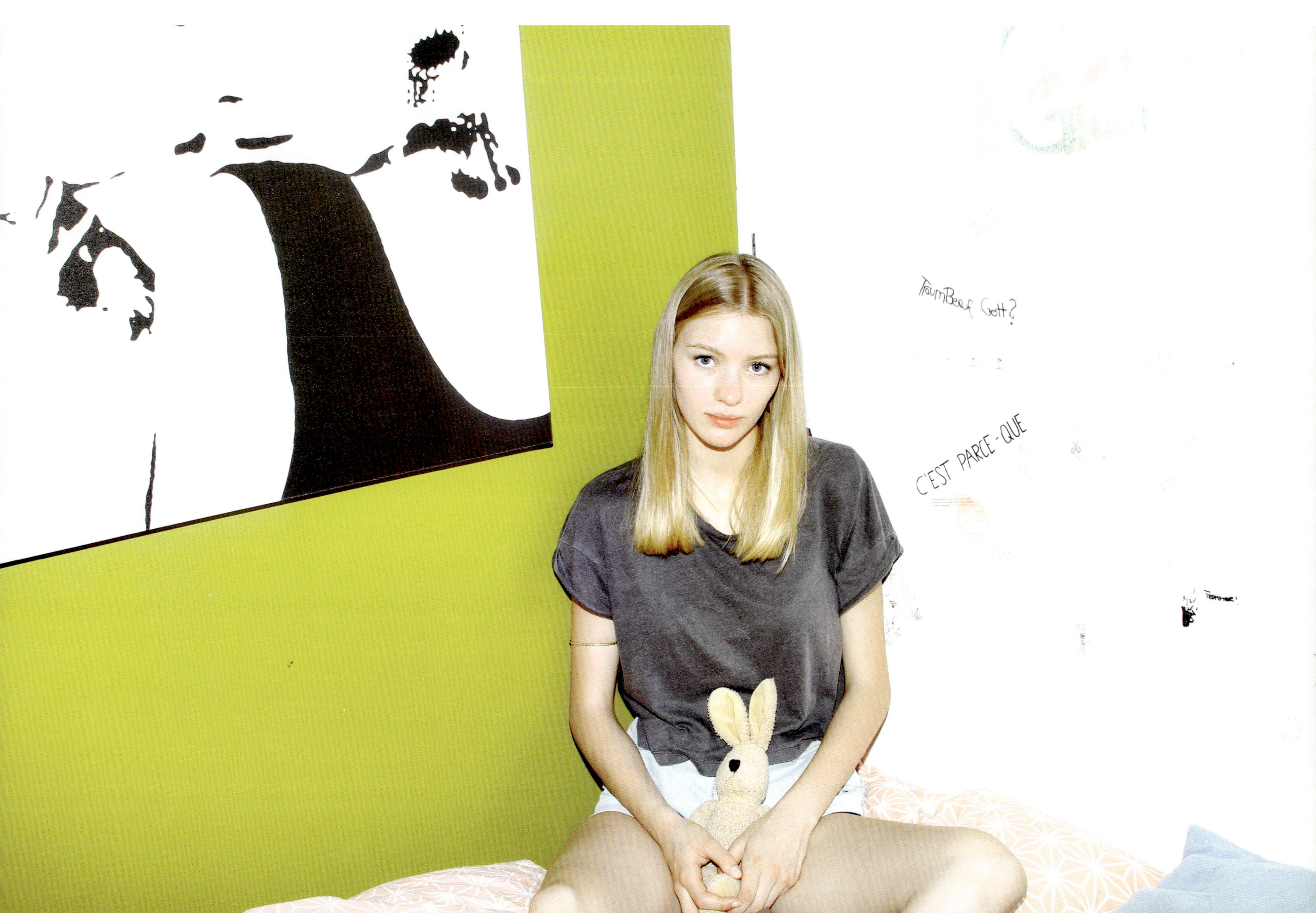
TraumBeruf Gott?
C'EST PARCE-QUE

Nicola at his parents', 2015
Upper West Side, New York City

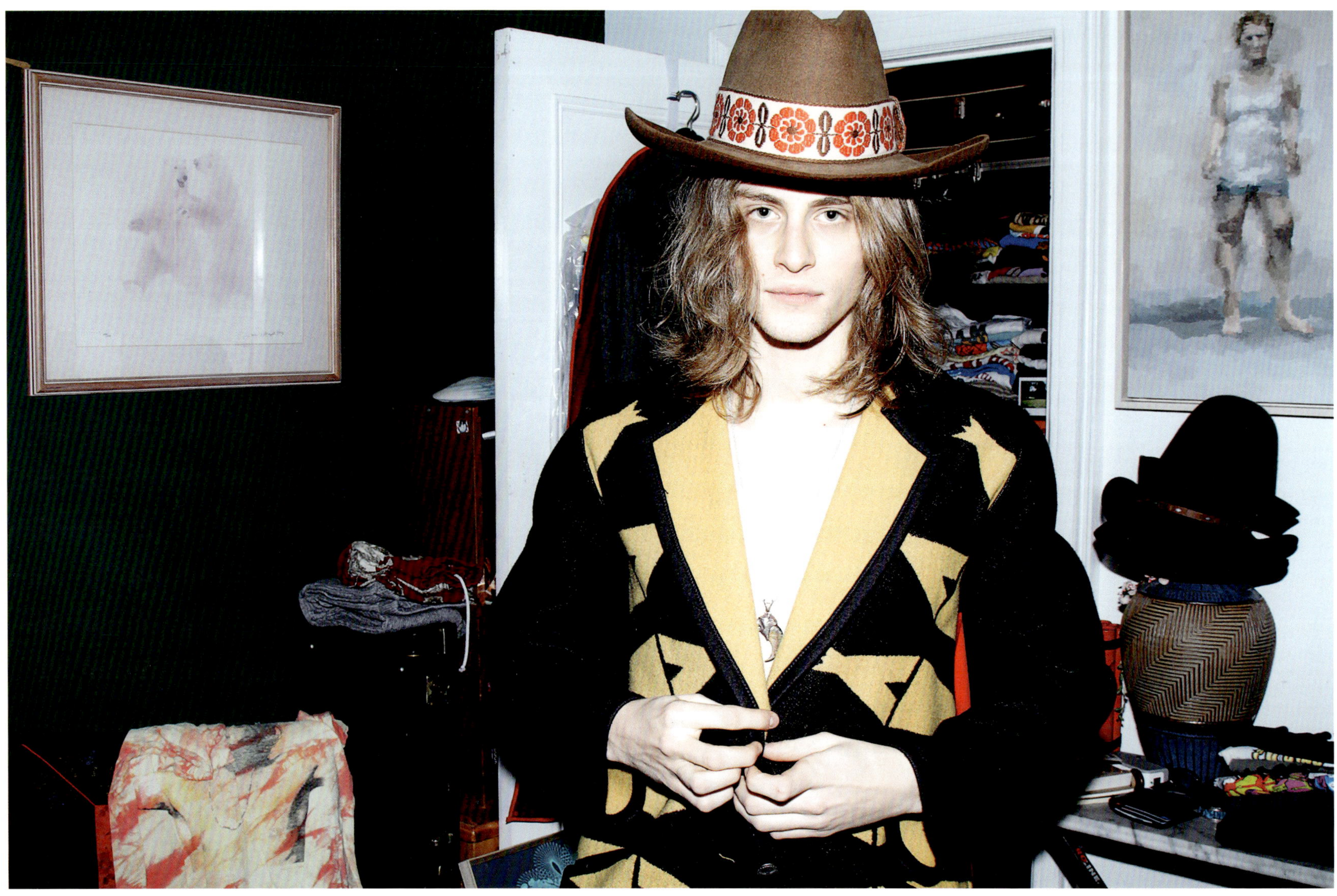

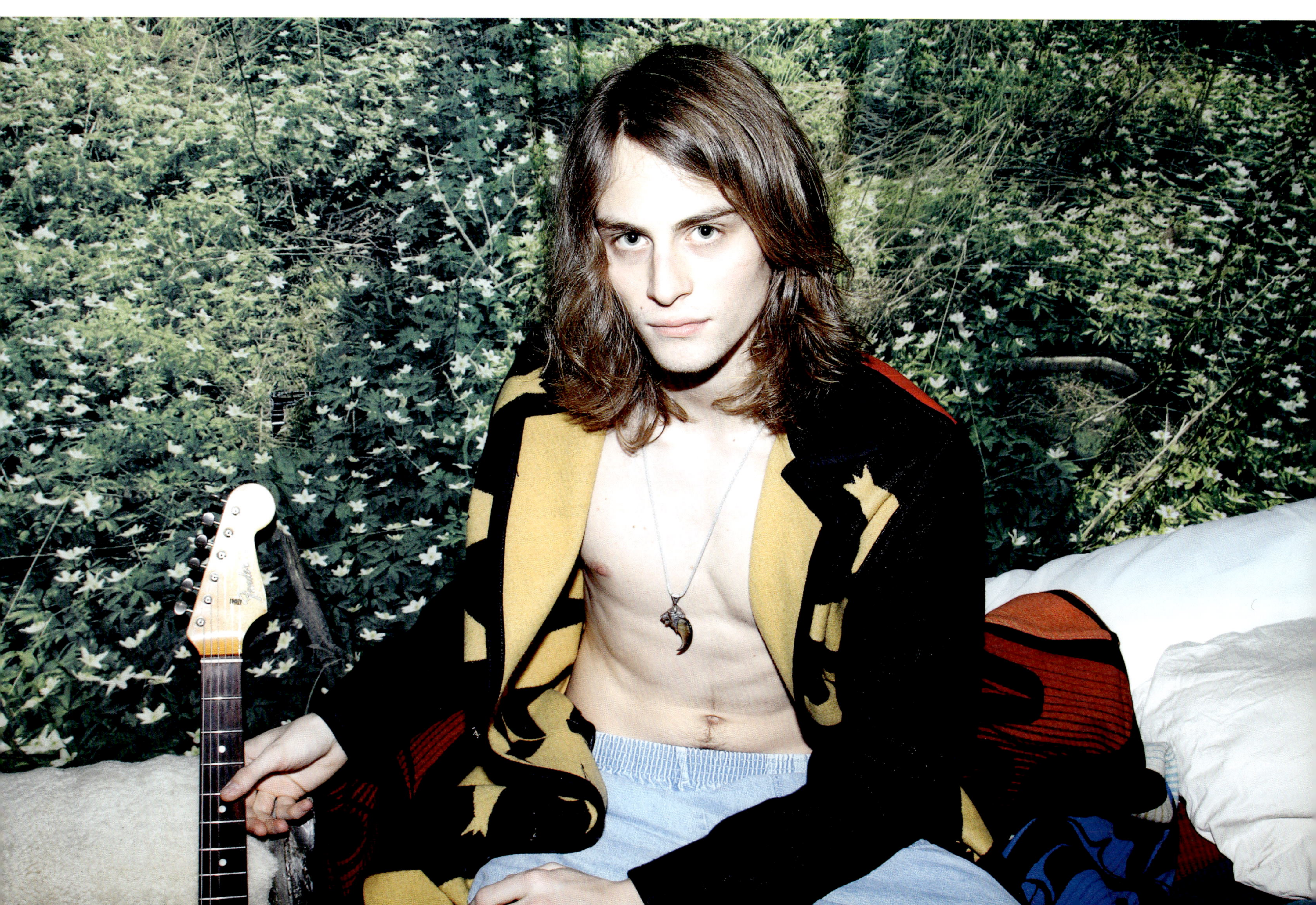

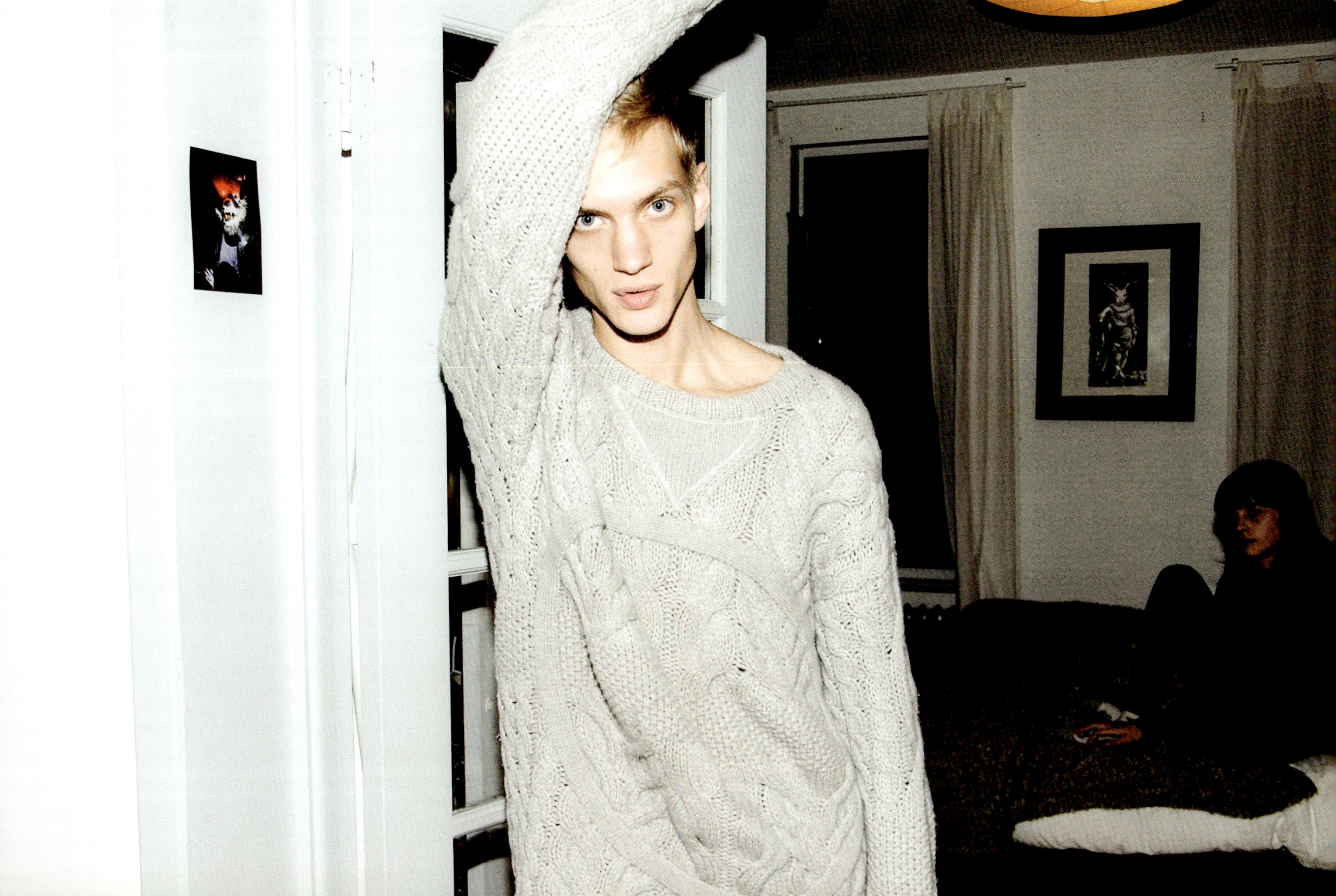

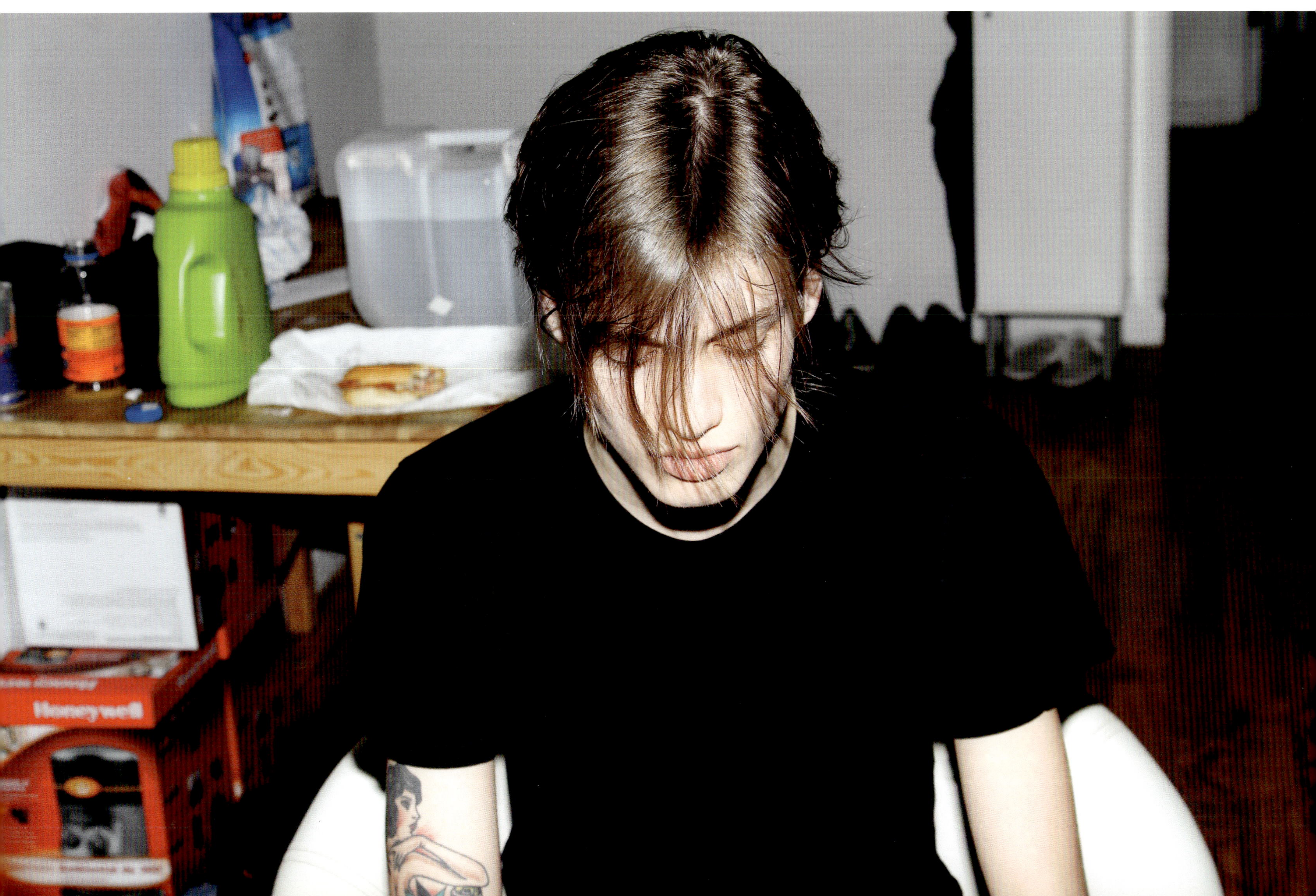

Bushwick, New York City

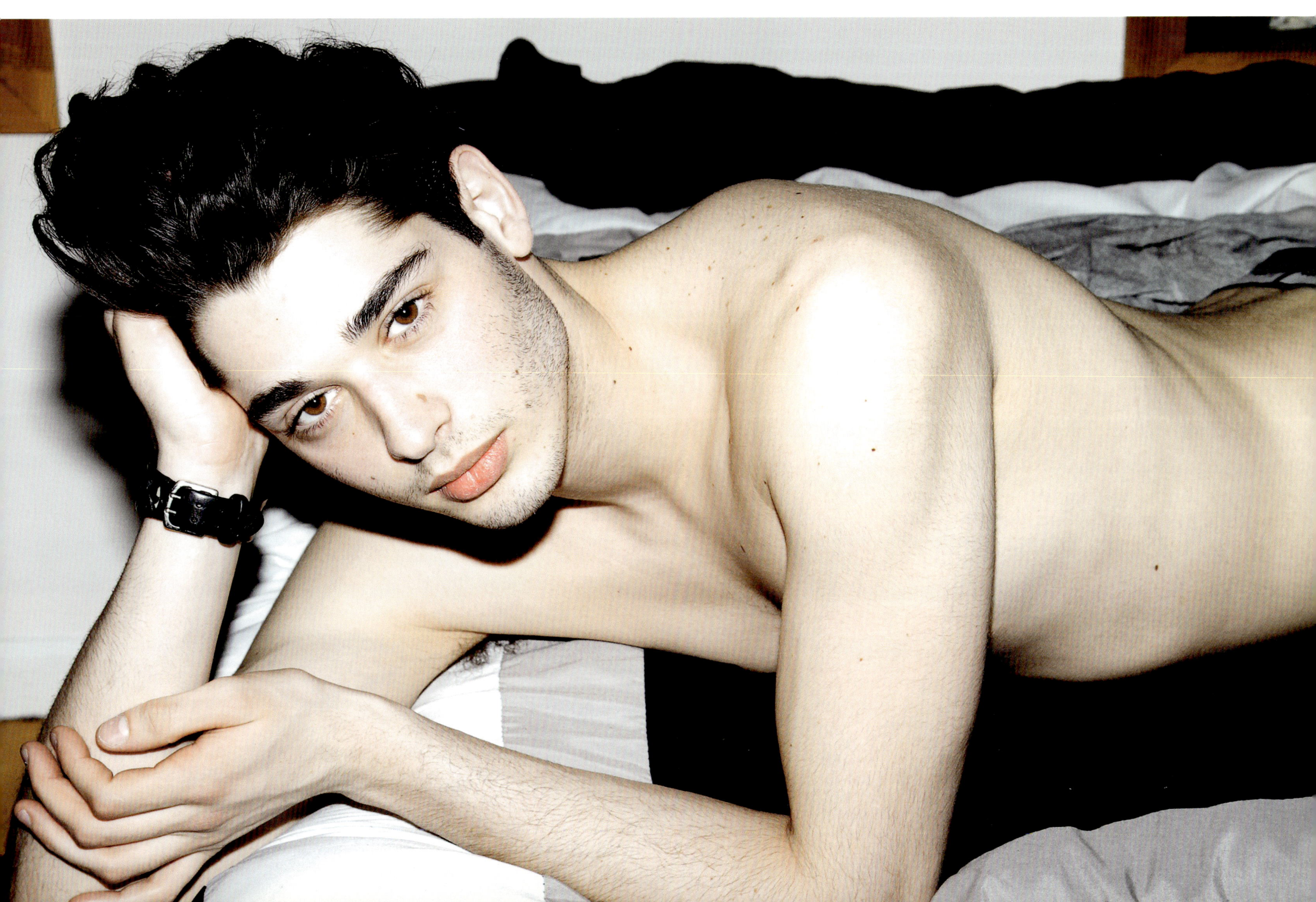

Best friends, 2009
New York City

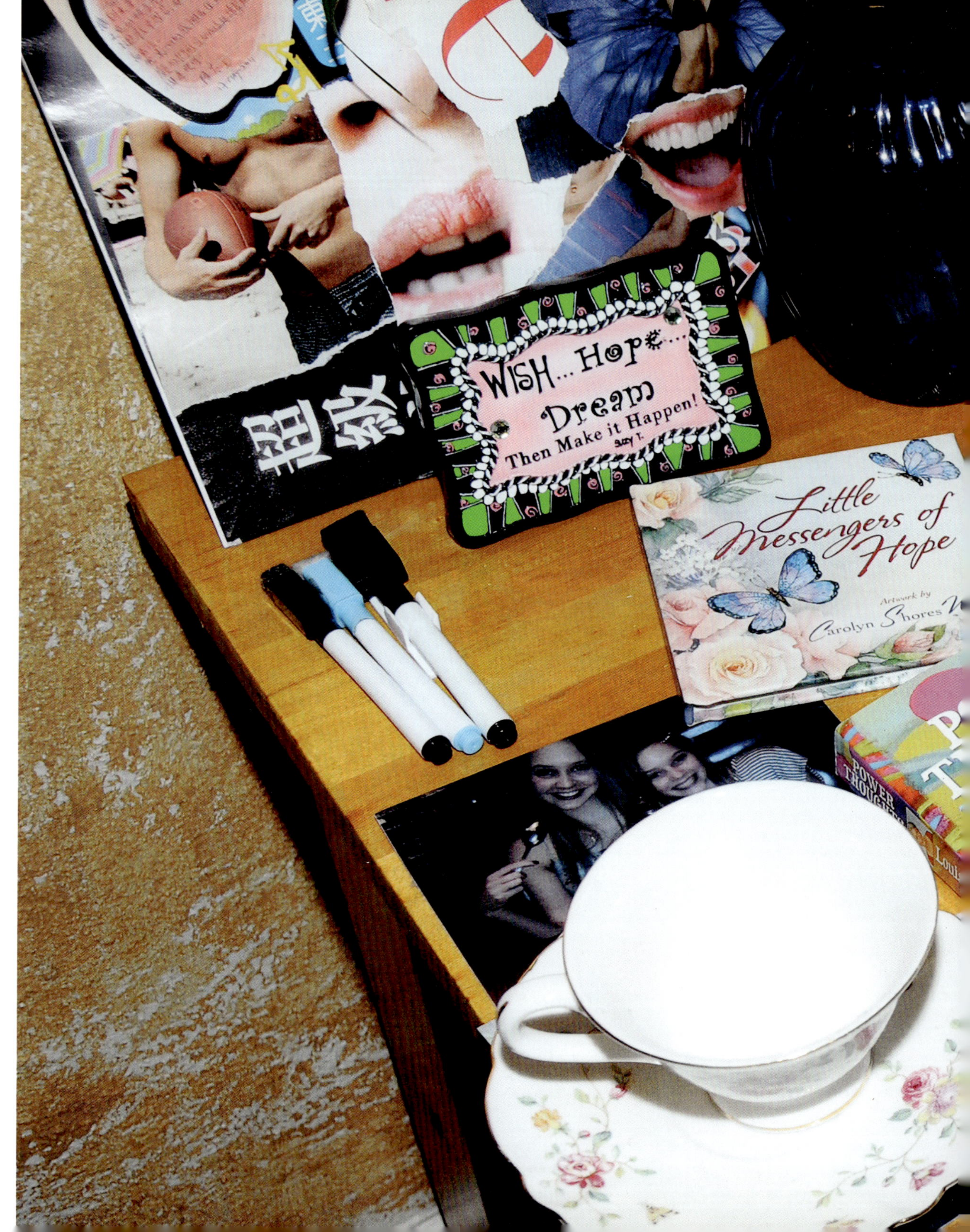

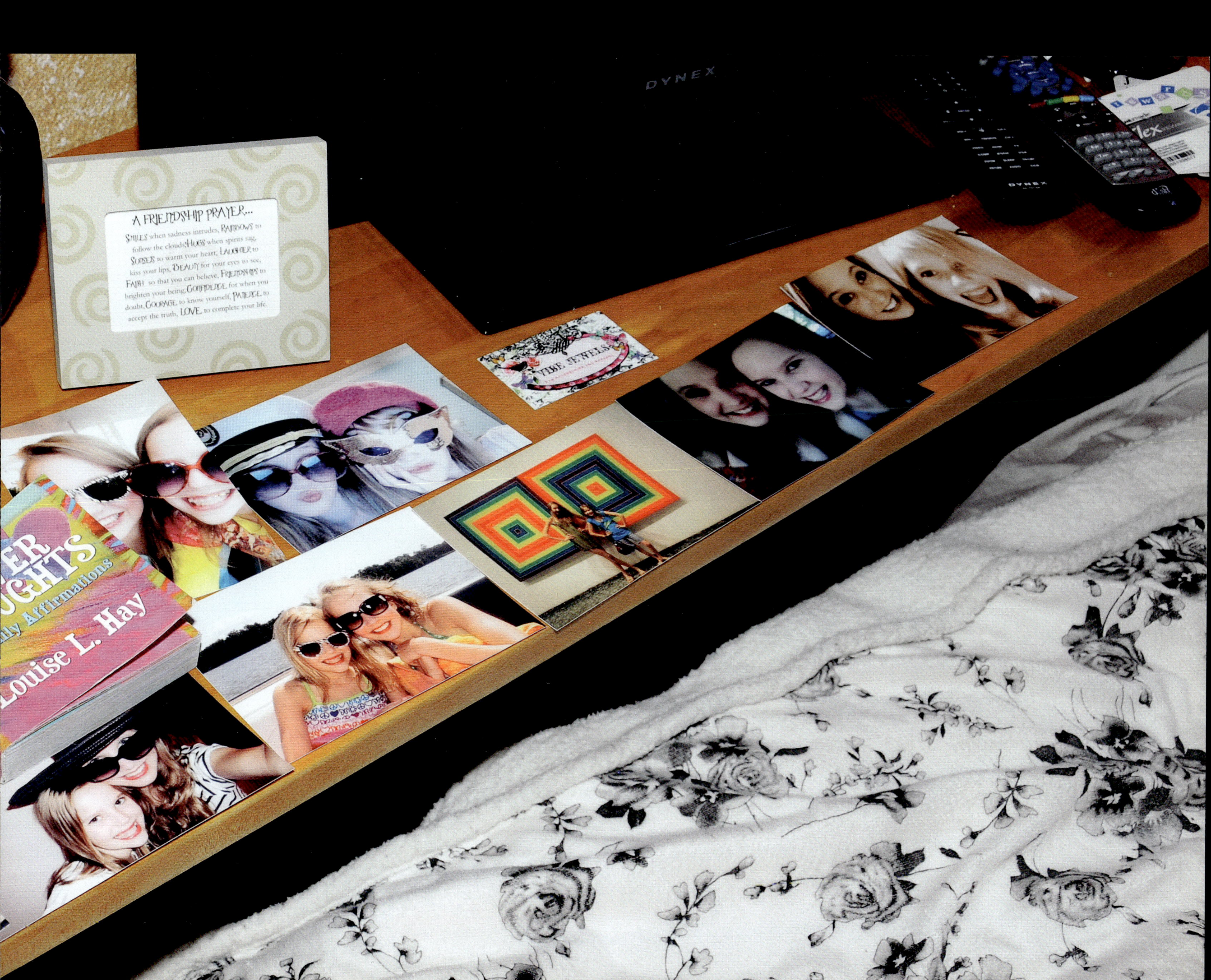
DYNEX
A FRIENDSHIP PRAYER...
VIBE JEWELS
Louise L. Hay

Sreffi & Heather, 2009
New York City

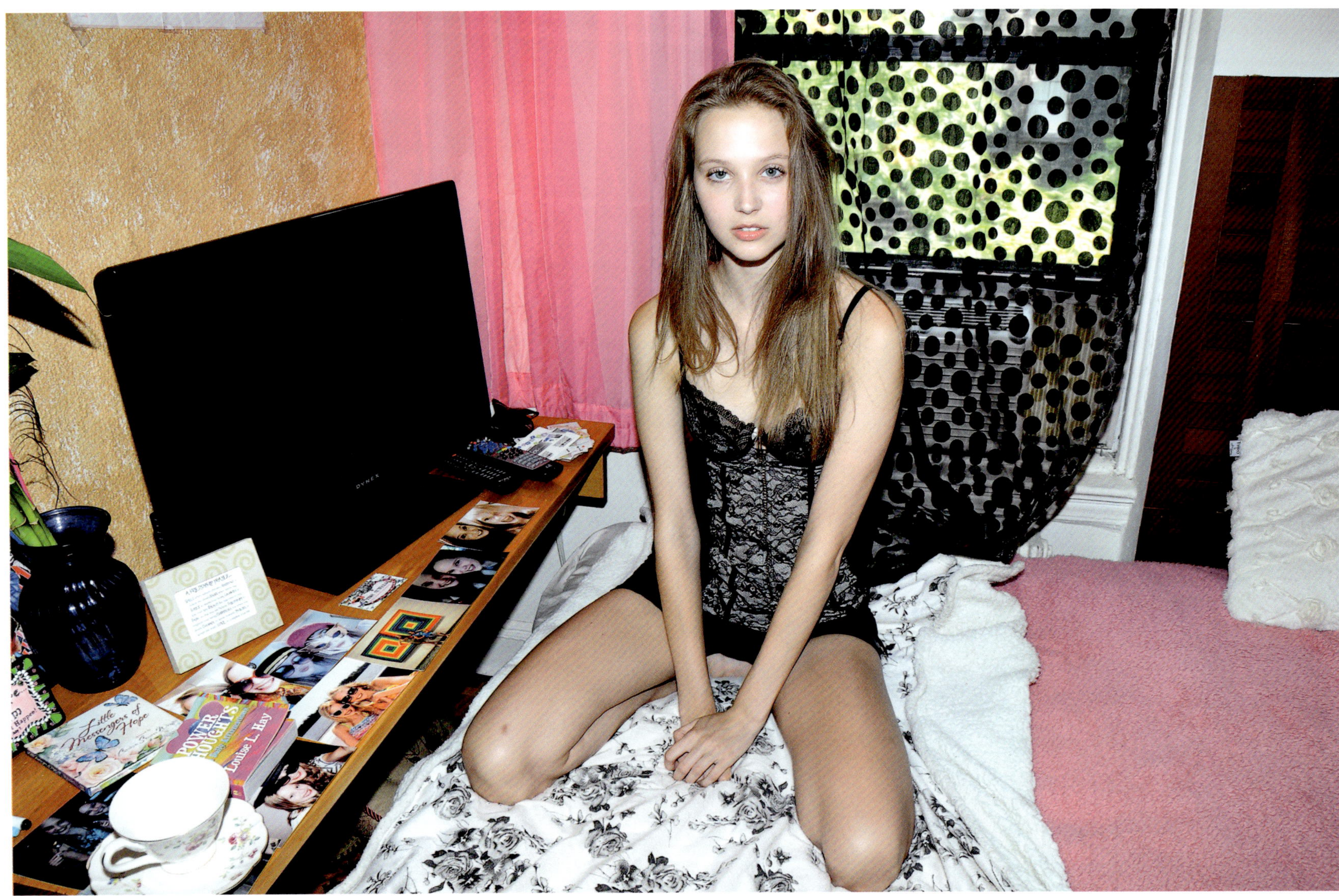

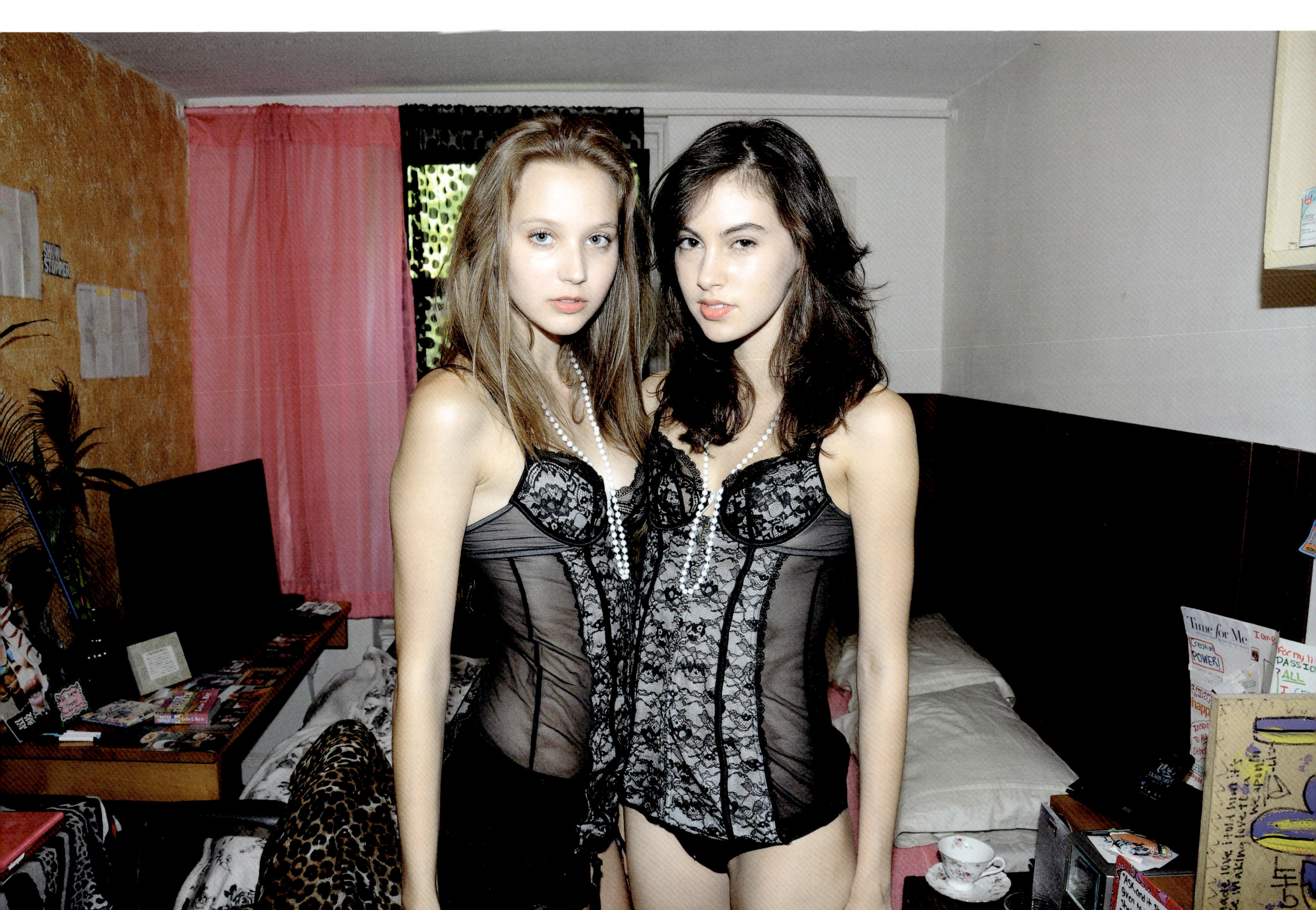

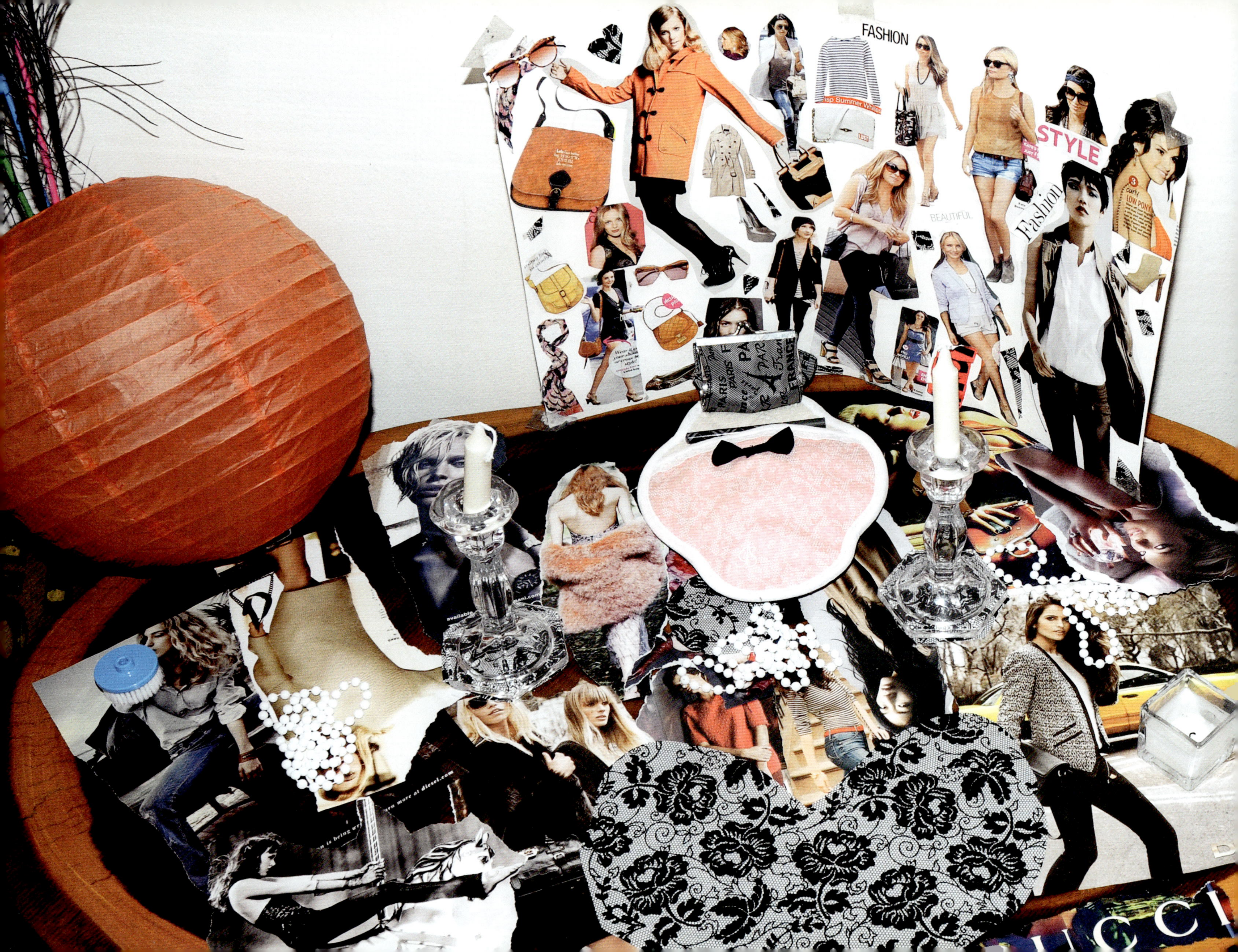
FASHION
STYLE
Fashion
BEAUTIFUL
LOW PONY
GUCCI

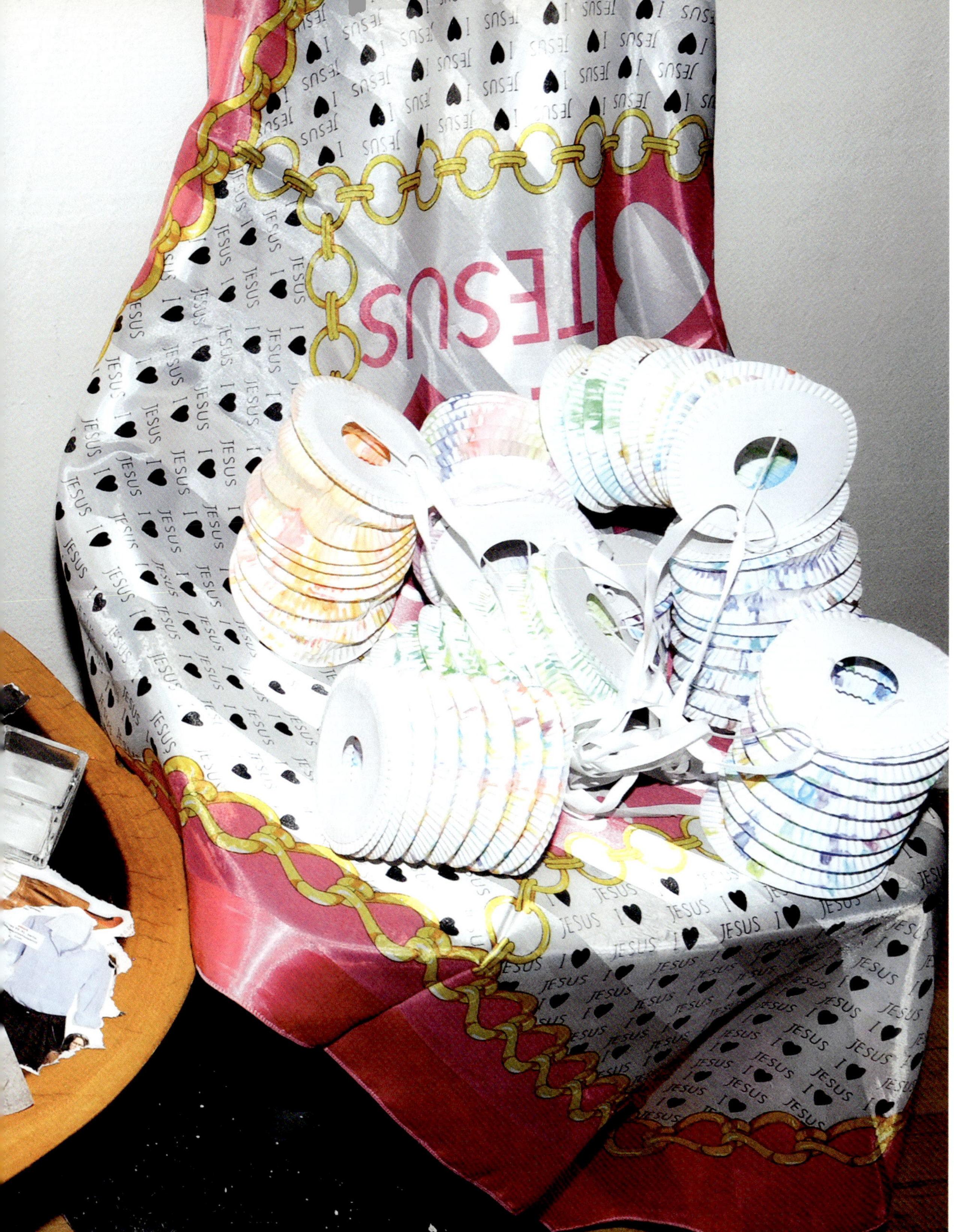

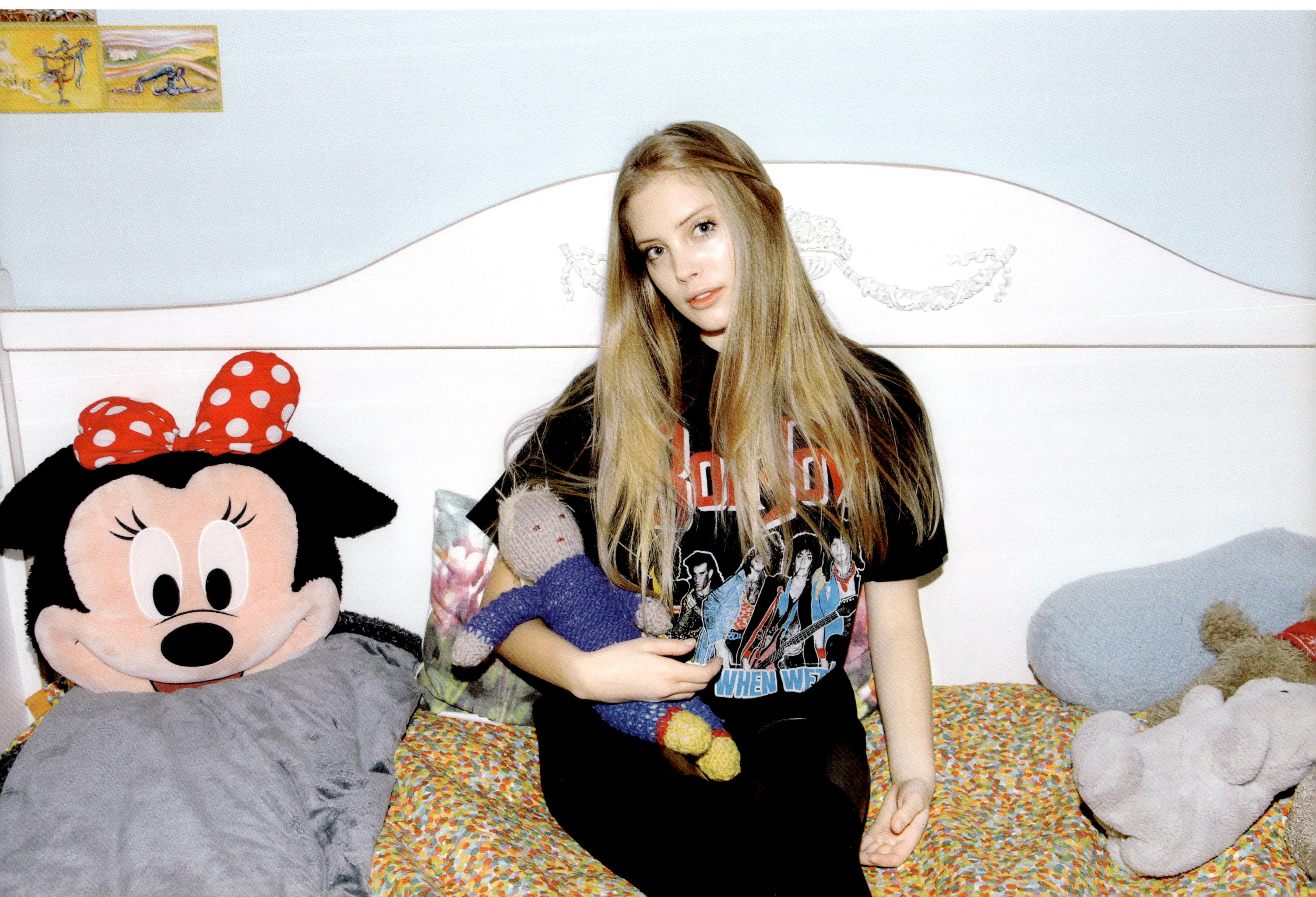

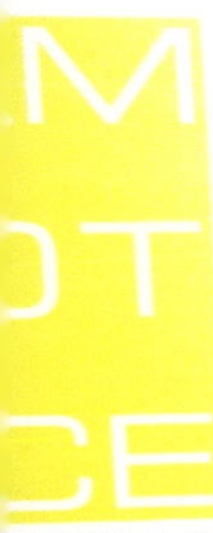

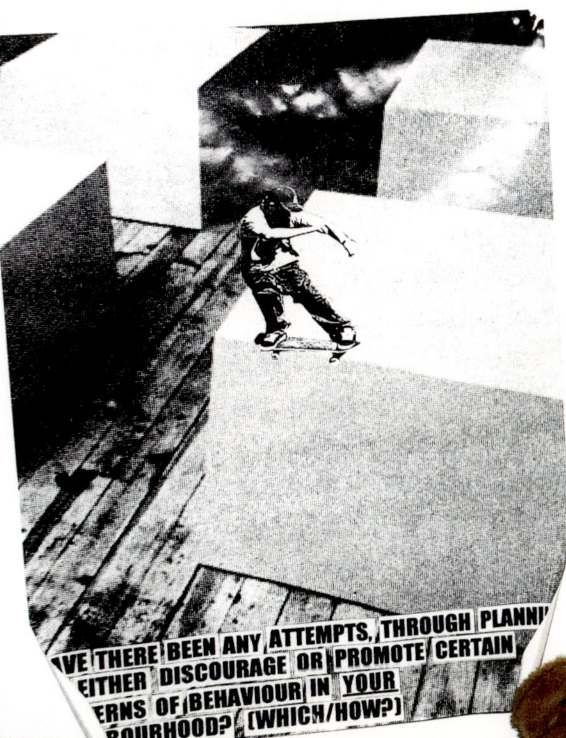
VE THERE BEEN ANY ATTEMPTS, THROUGH PLANNI
EITHER DISCOURAGE OR PROMOTE CERTAIN
ERNS OF BEHAVIOUR IN YOUR
BOURHOOD? (WHICH/HOW?)

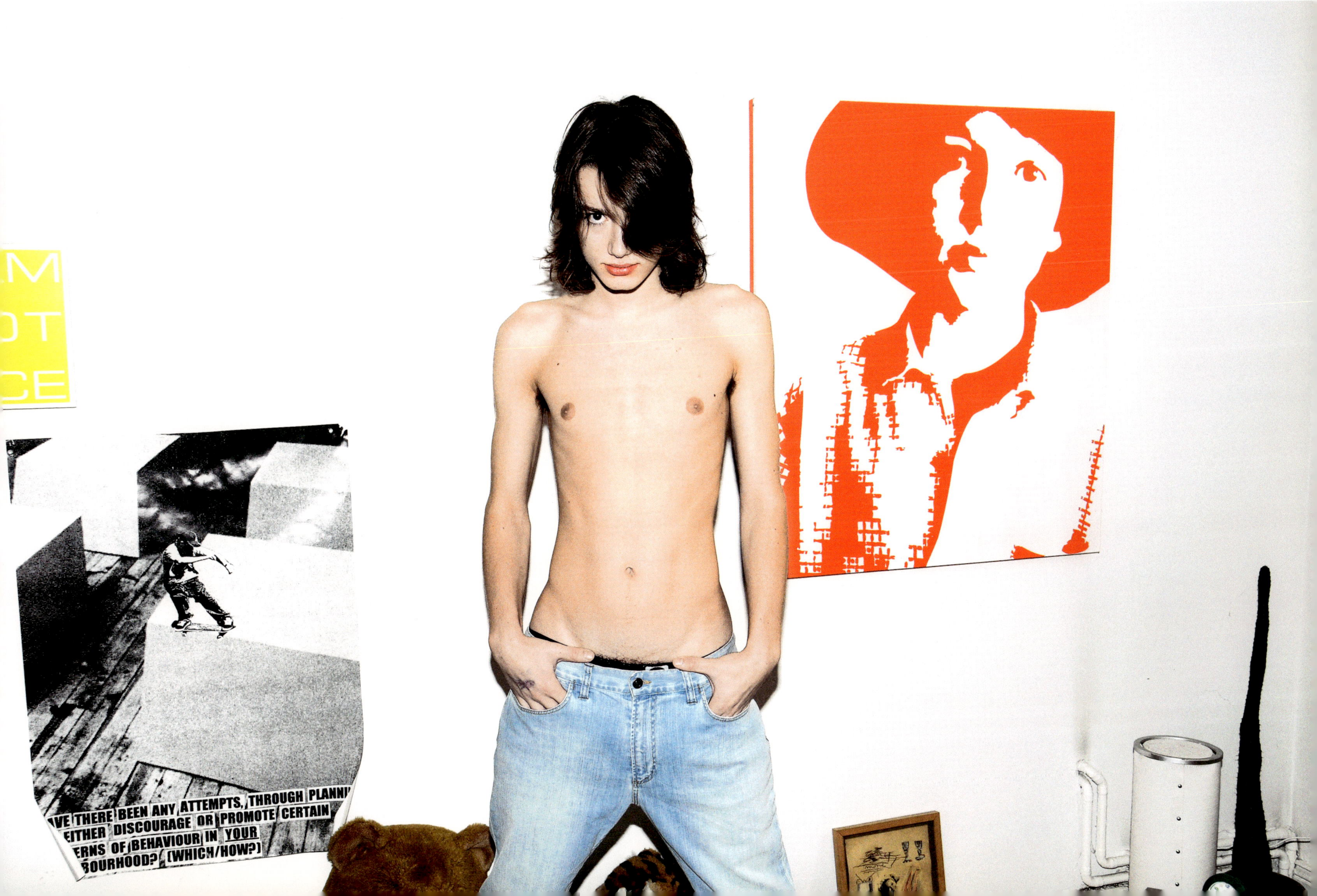

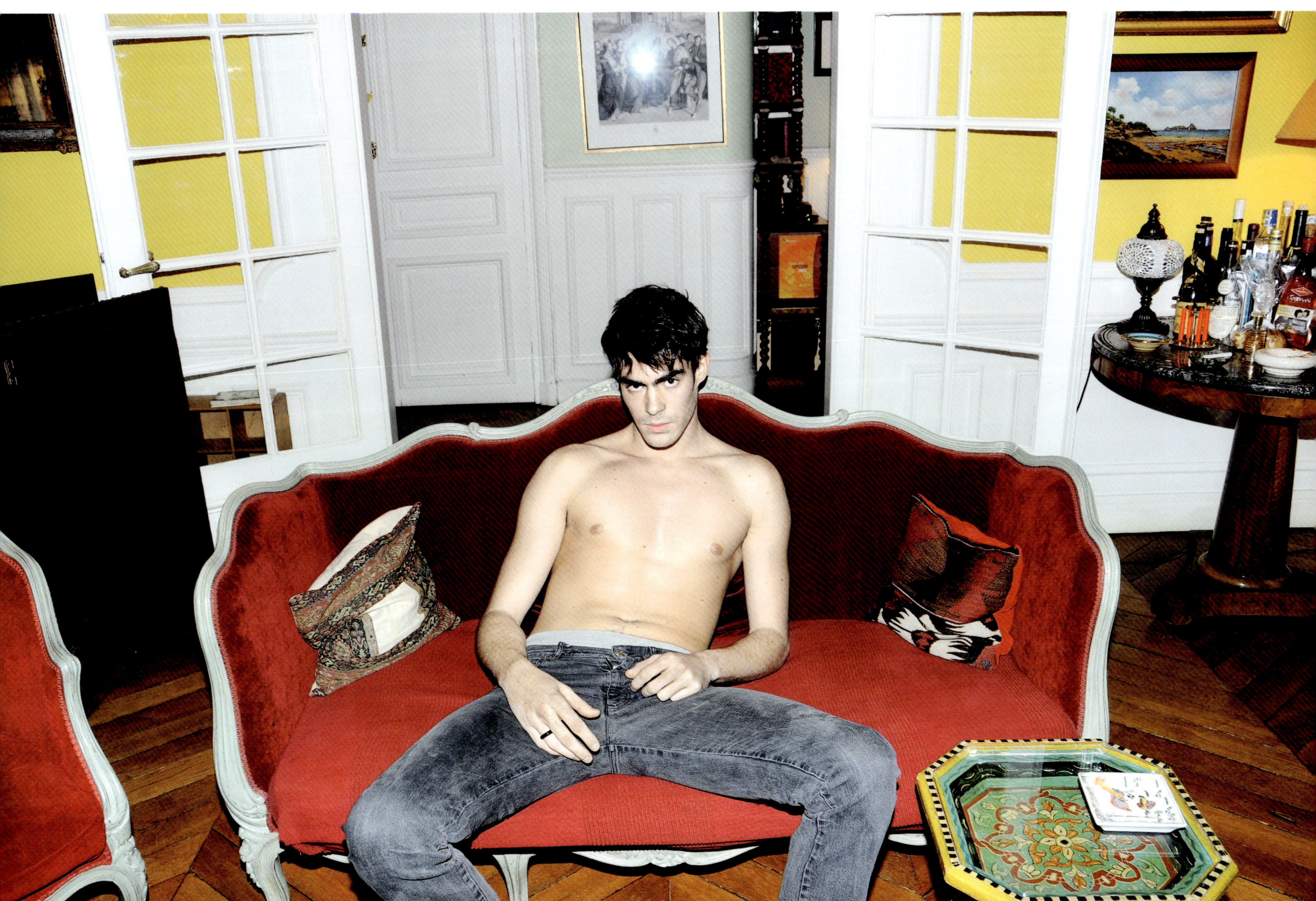

Leila, 2016
East Williamsburg, New York City

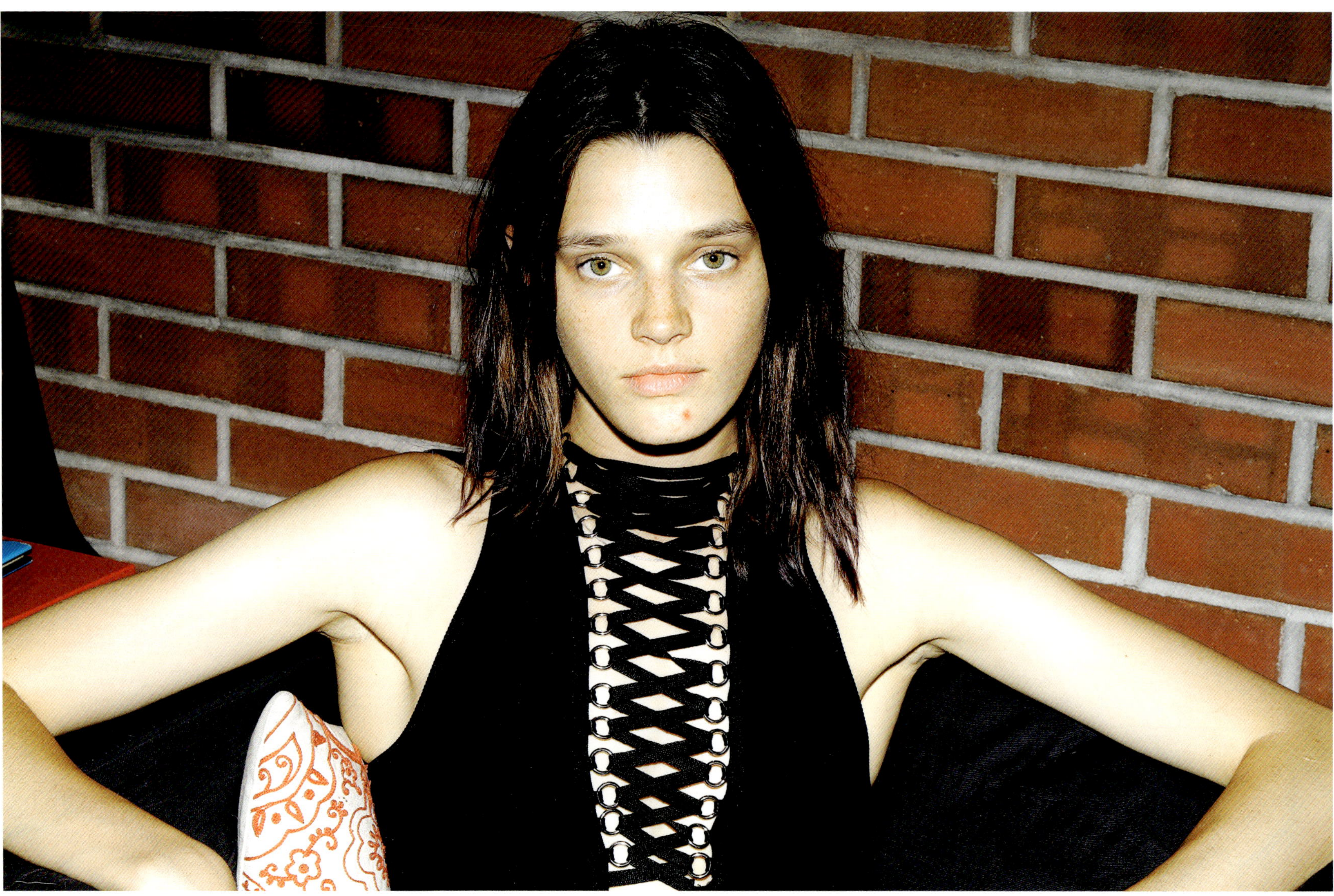

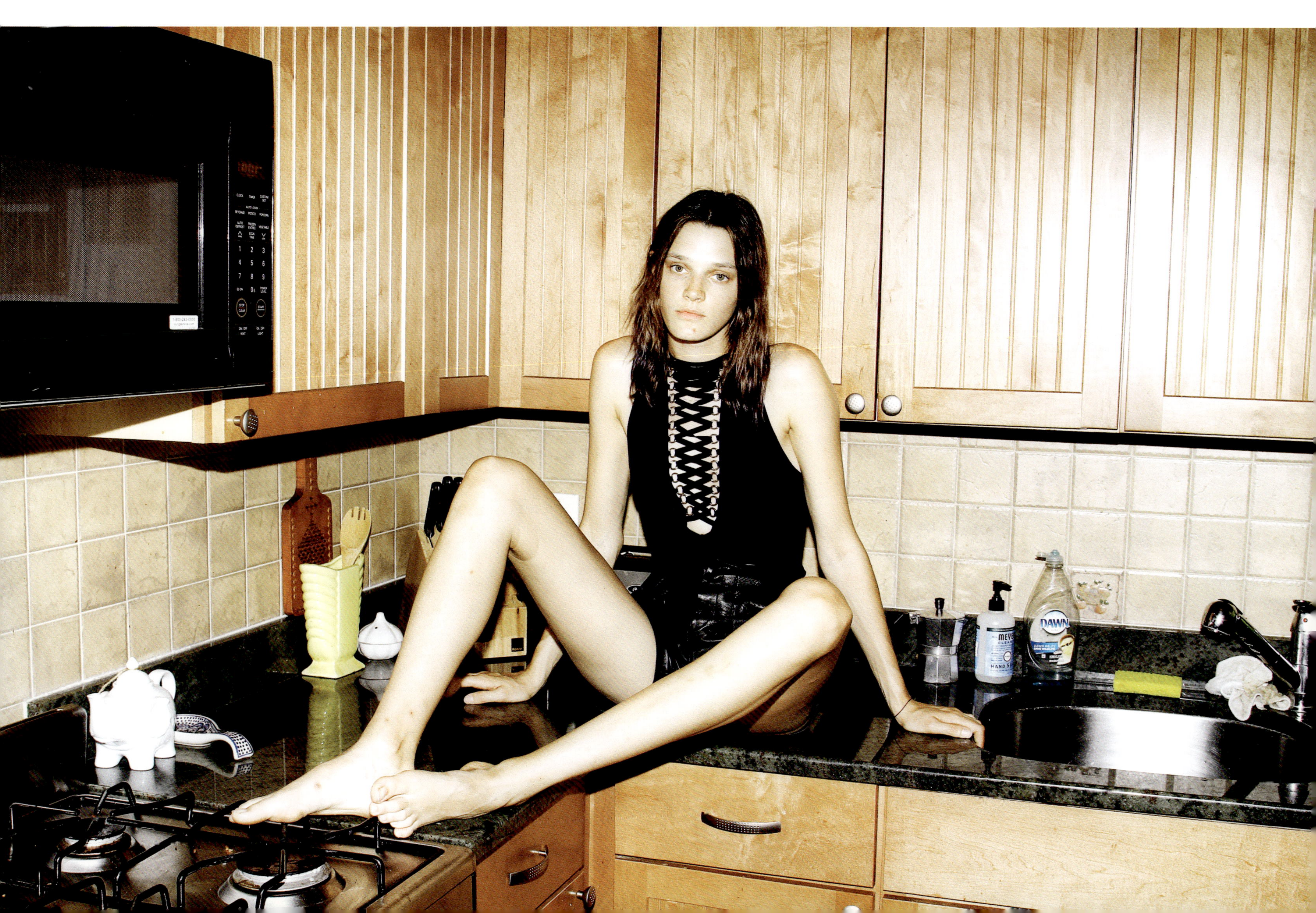

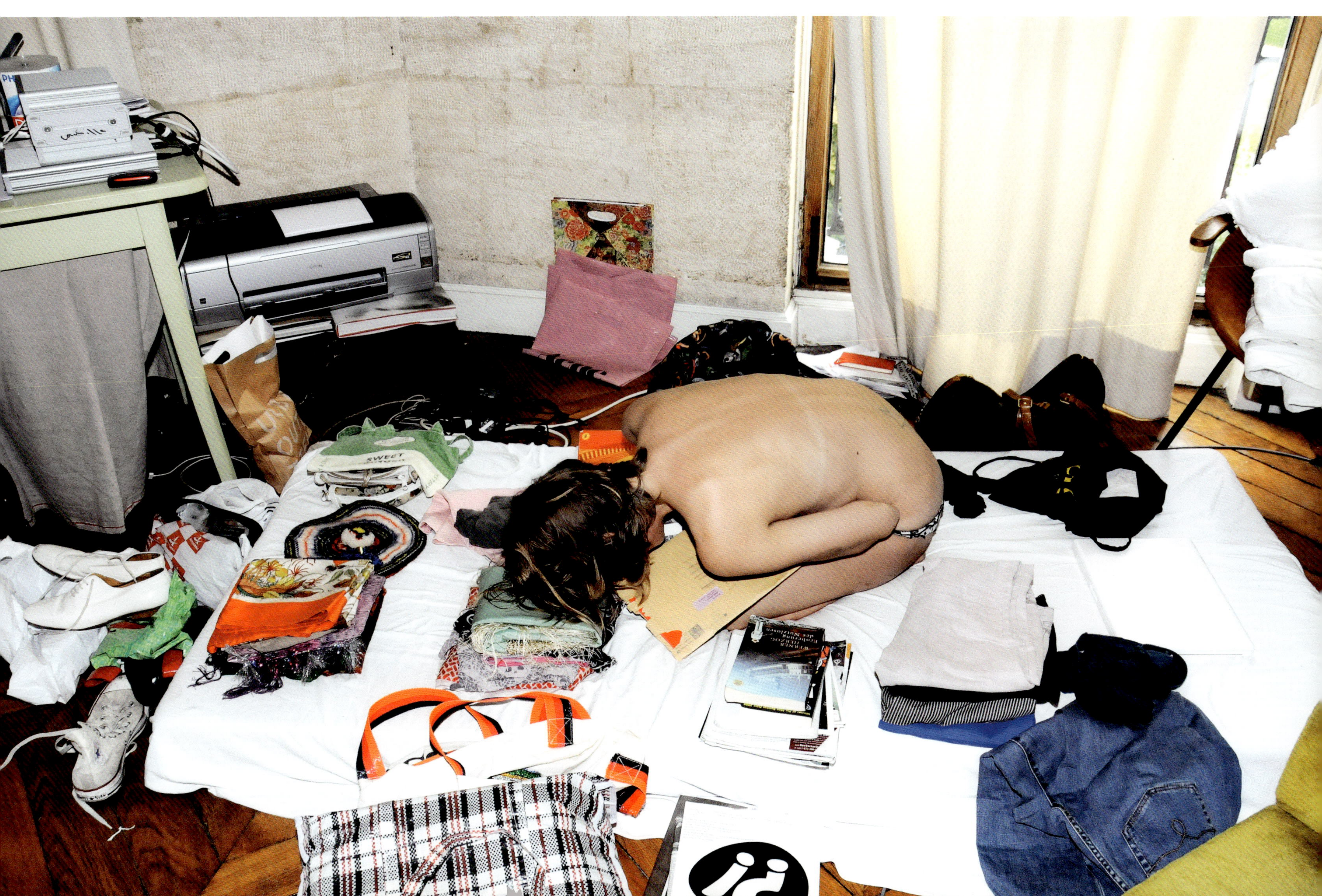

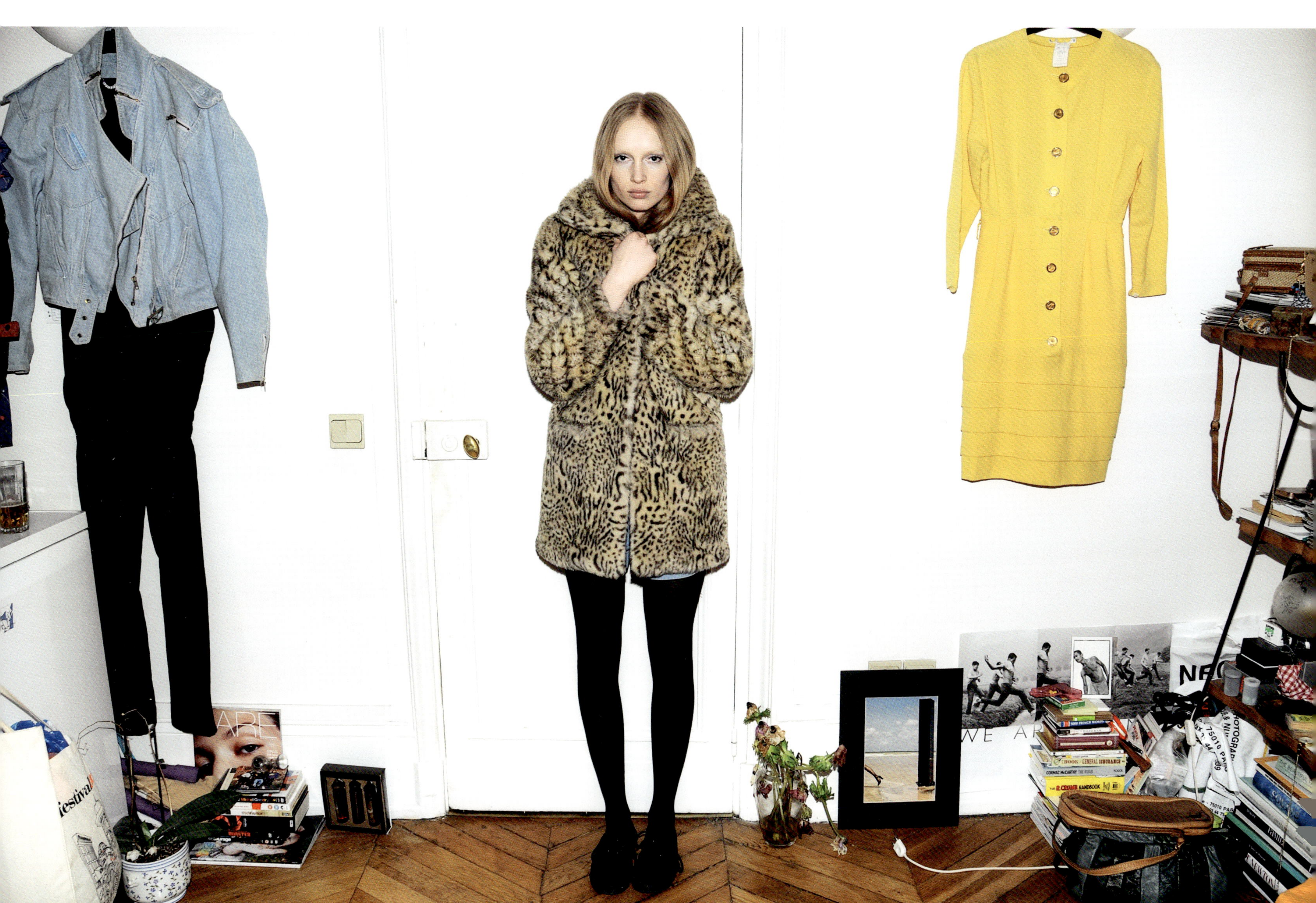

Bushwick, New York City

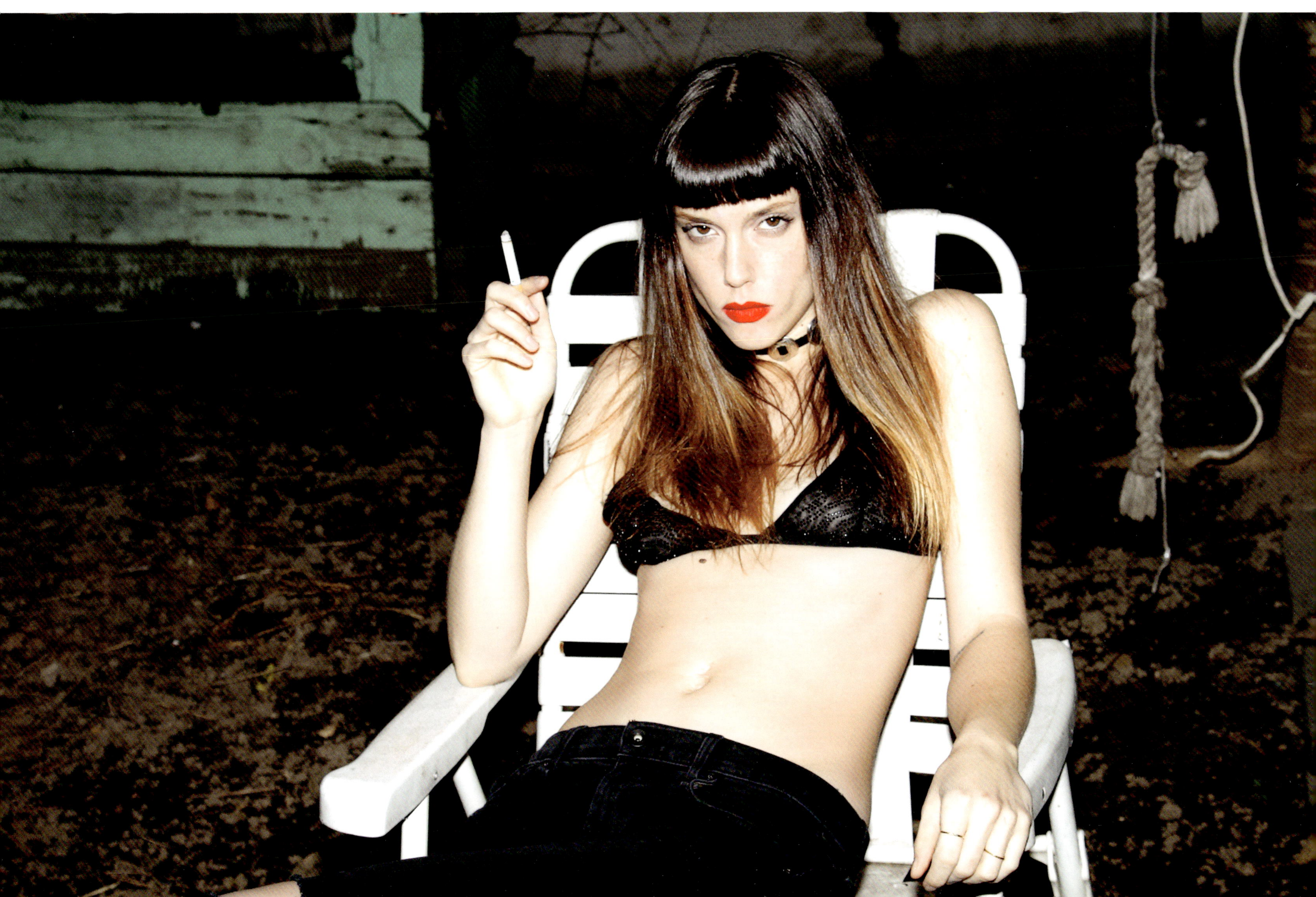

 Mateo at his uncle's, 2015
Jersey City

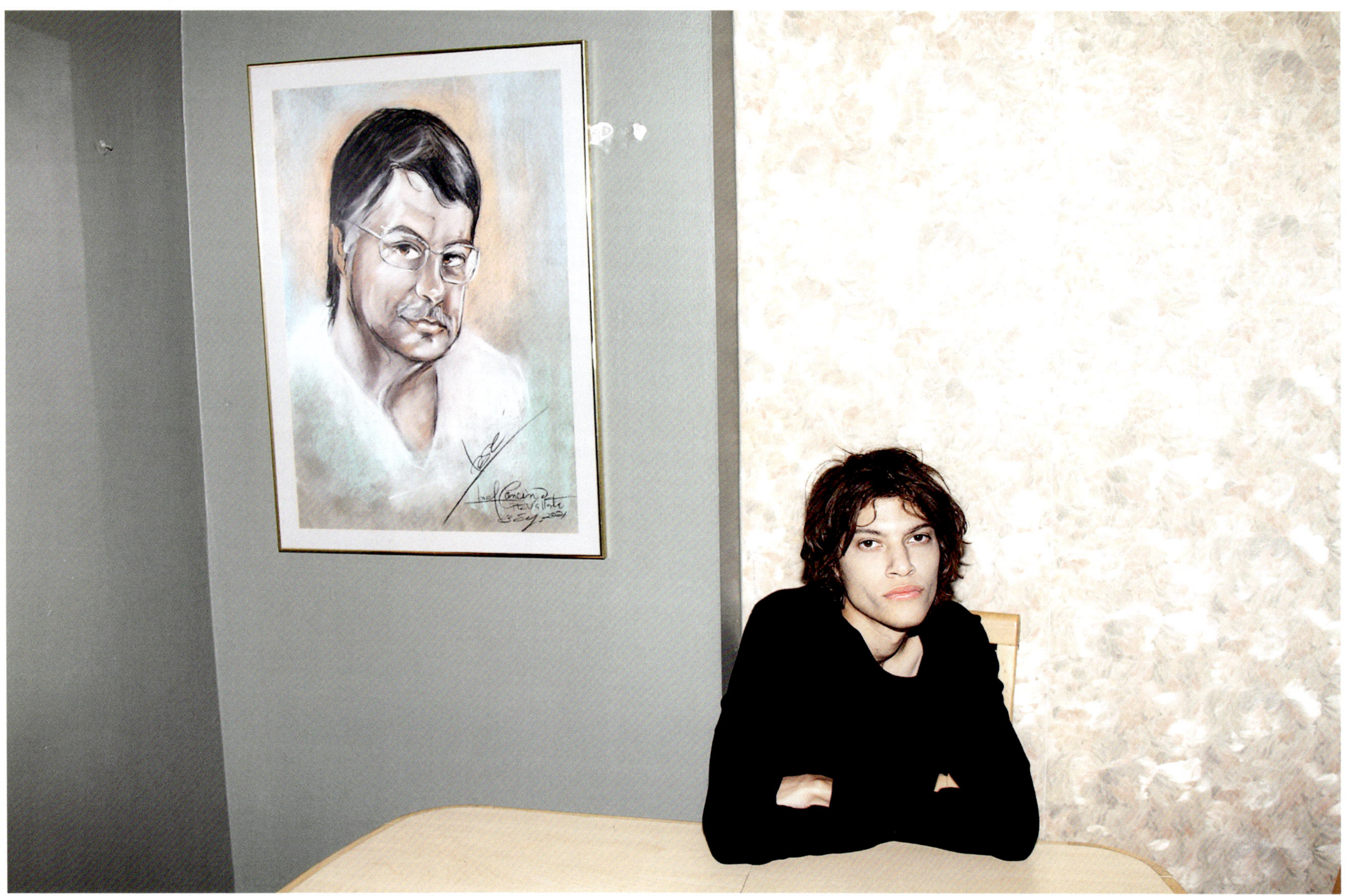

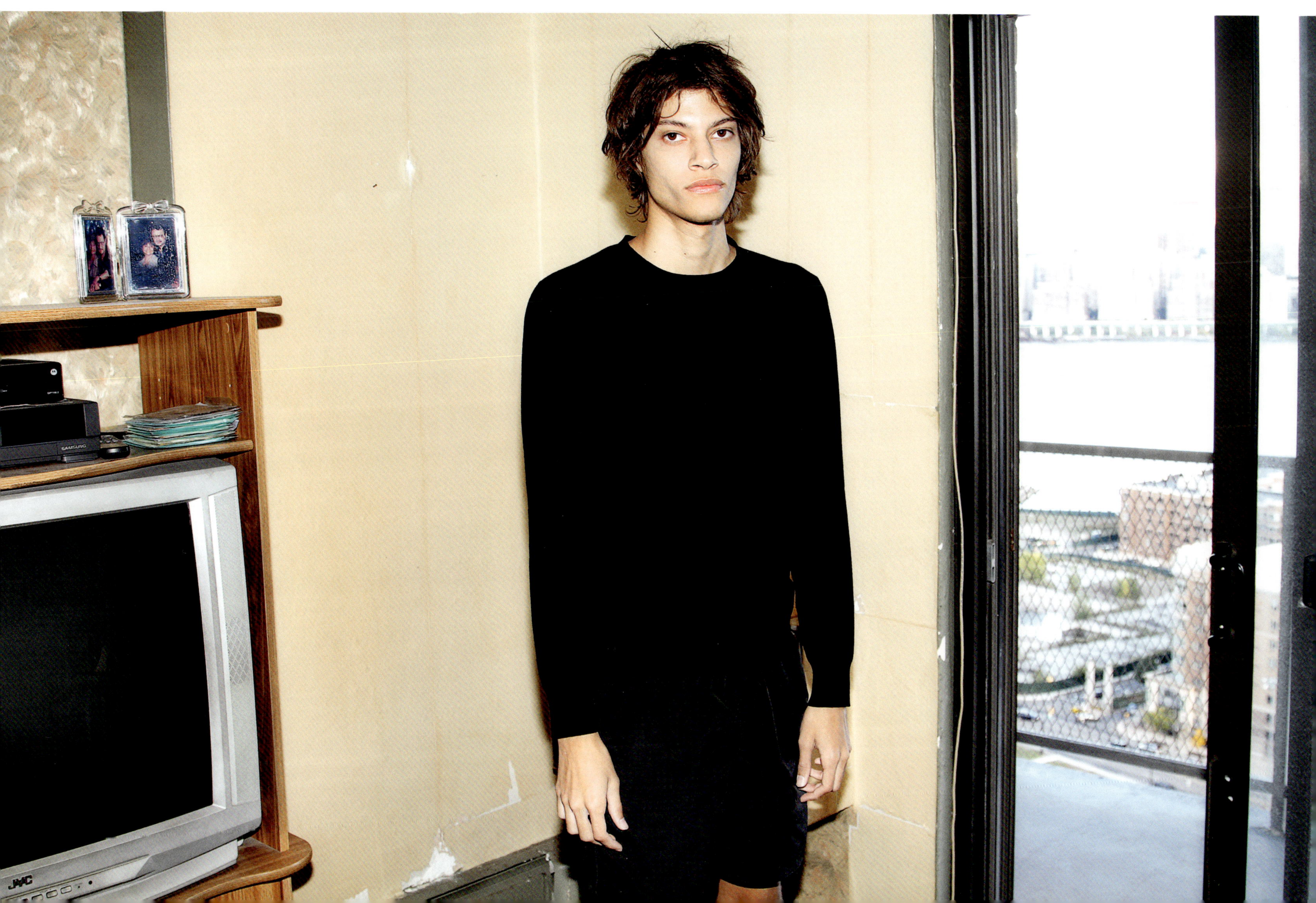

Prospect Park, New York City

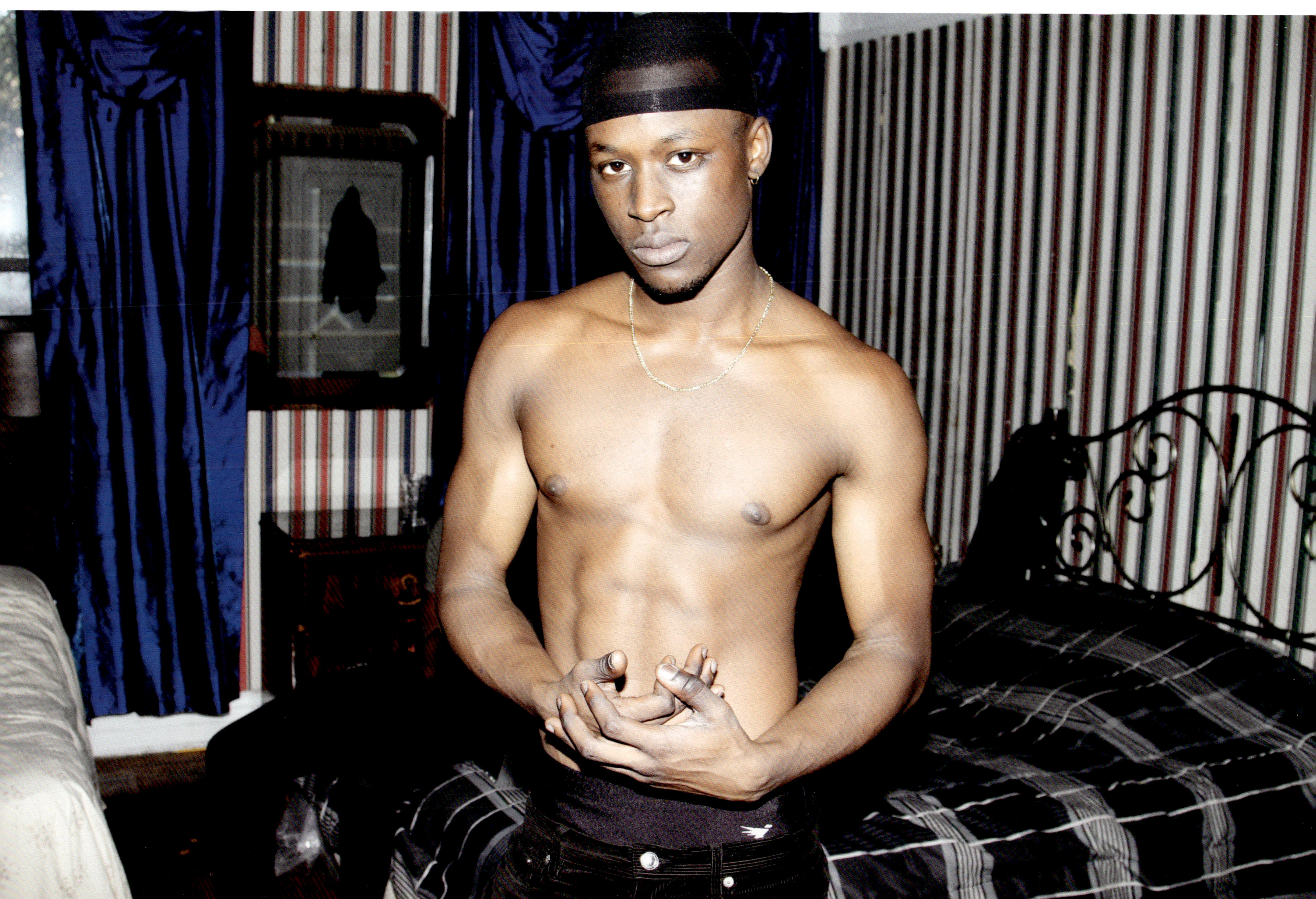

Khorey & Torey, 2015
Prospect Park, New York City

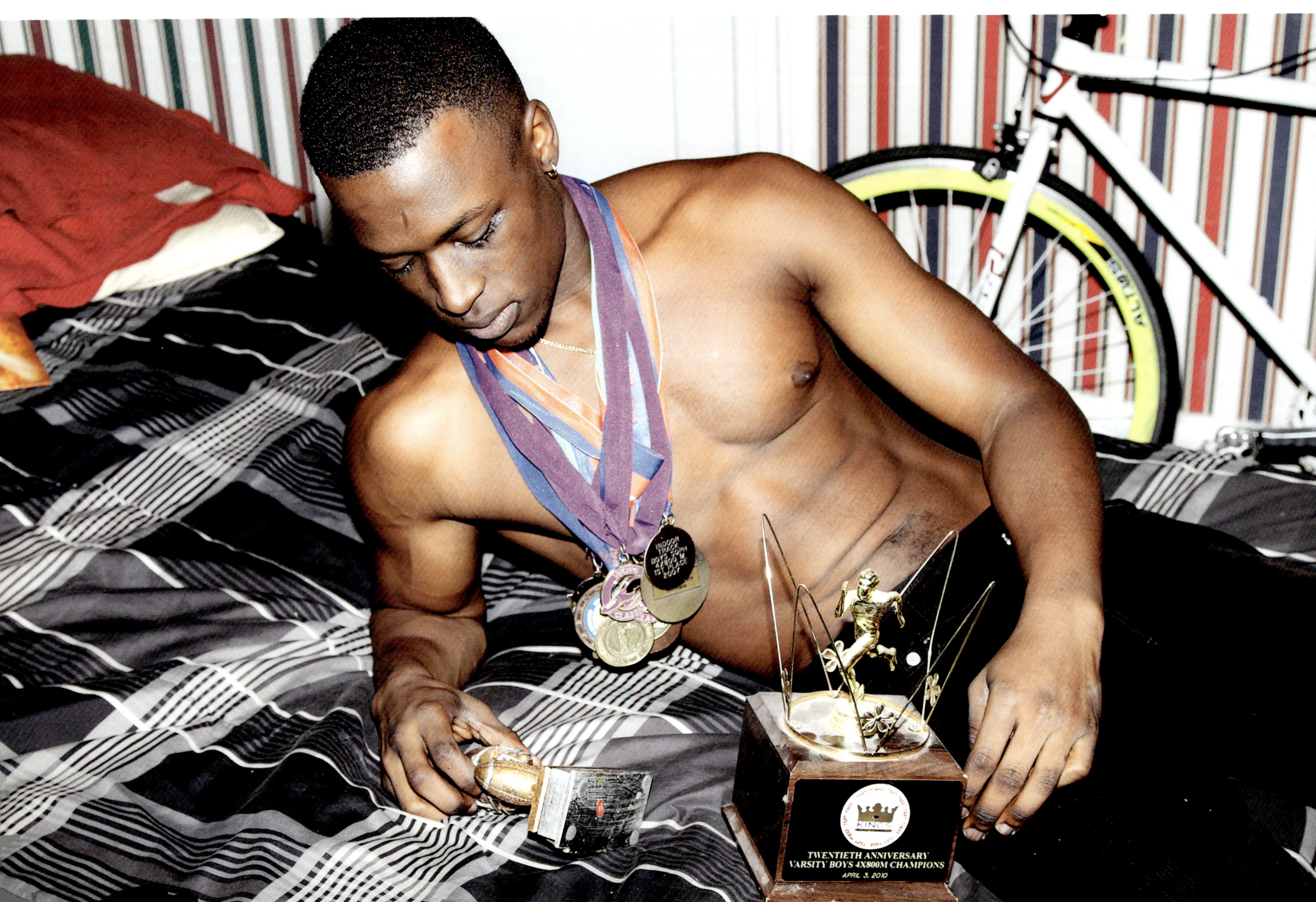

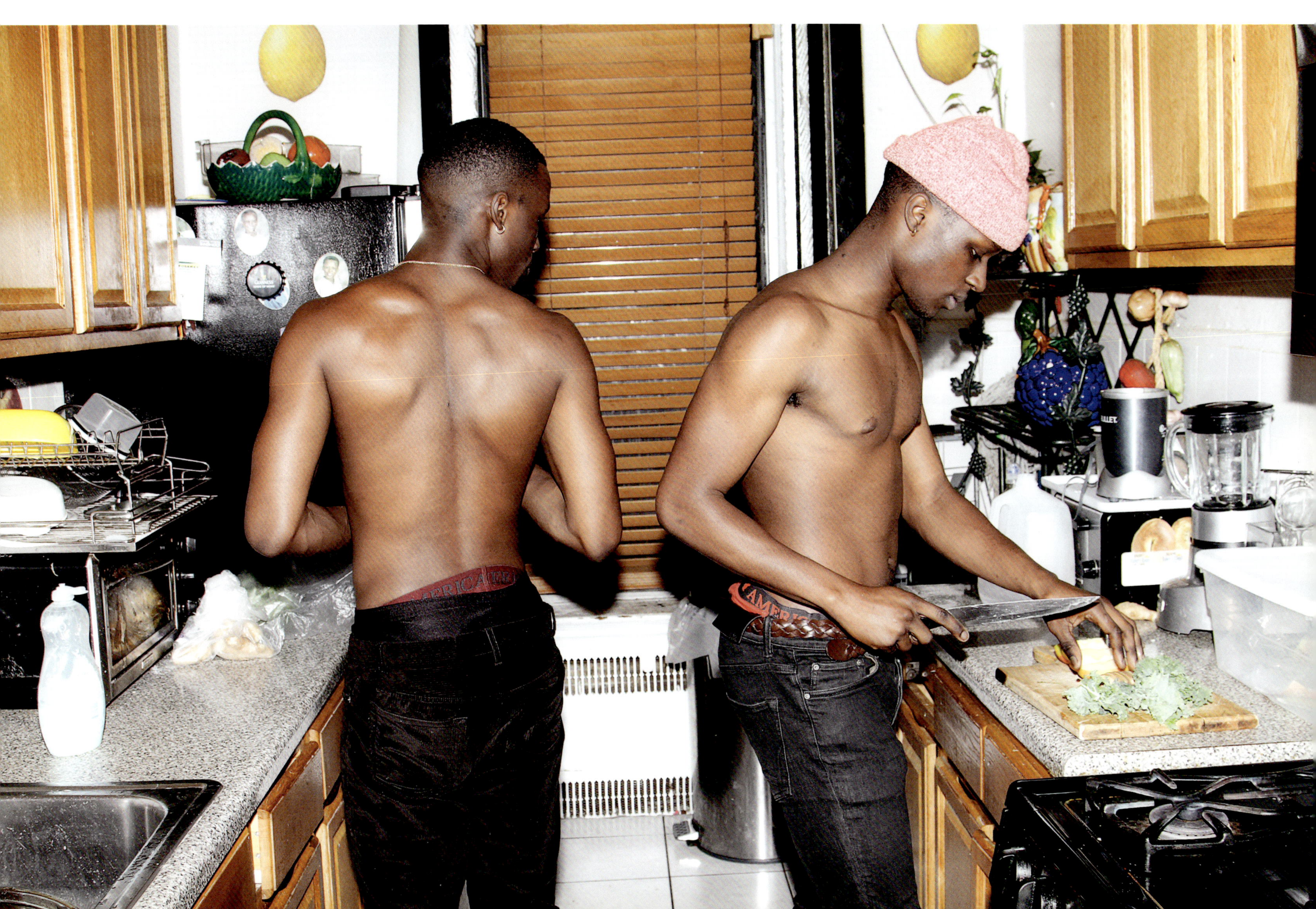

Harlem, New York City

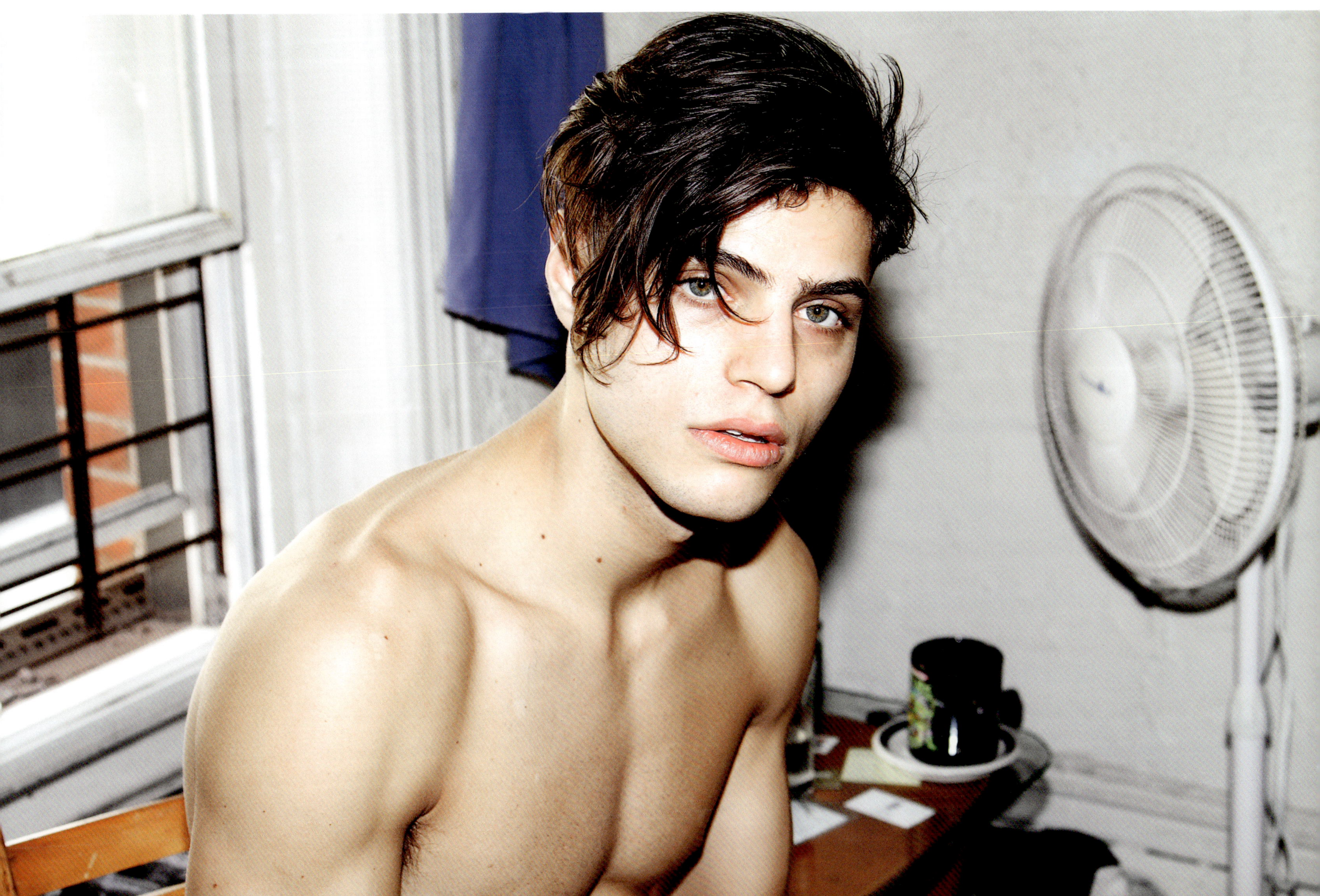

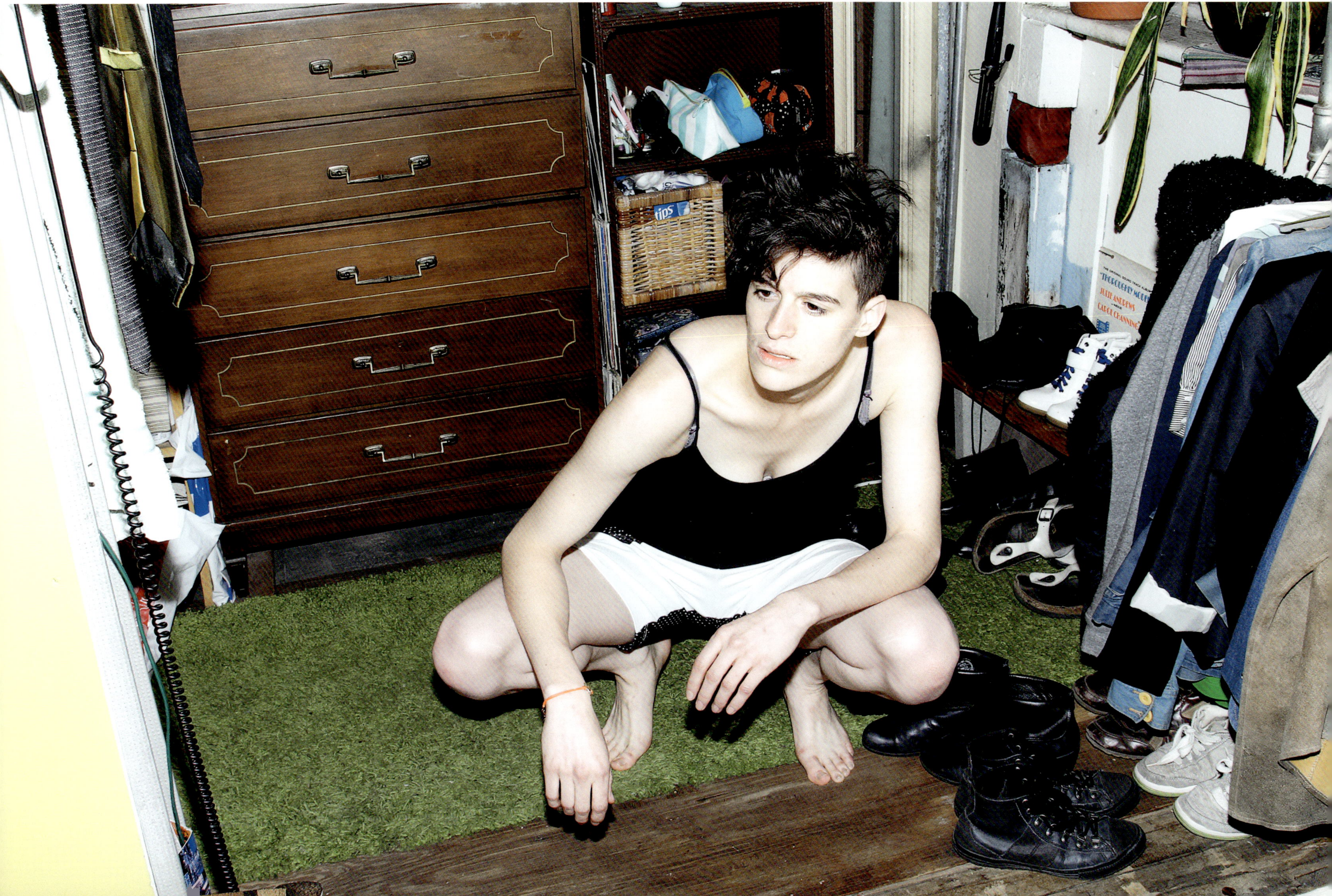

East Williamsburg, New York City

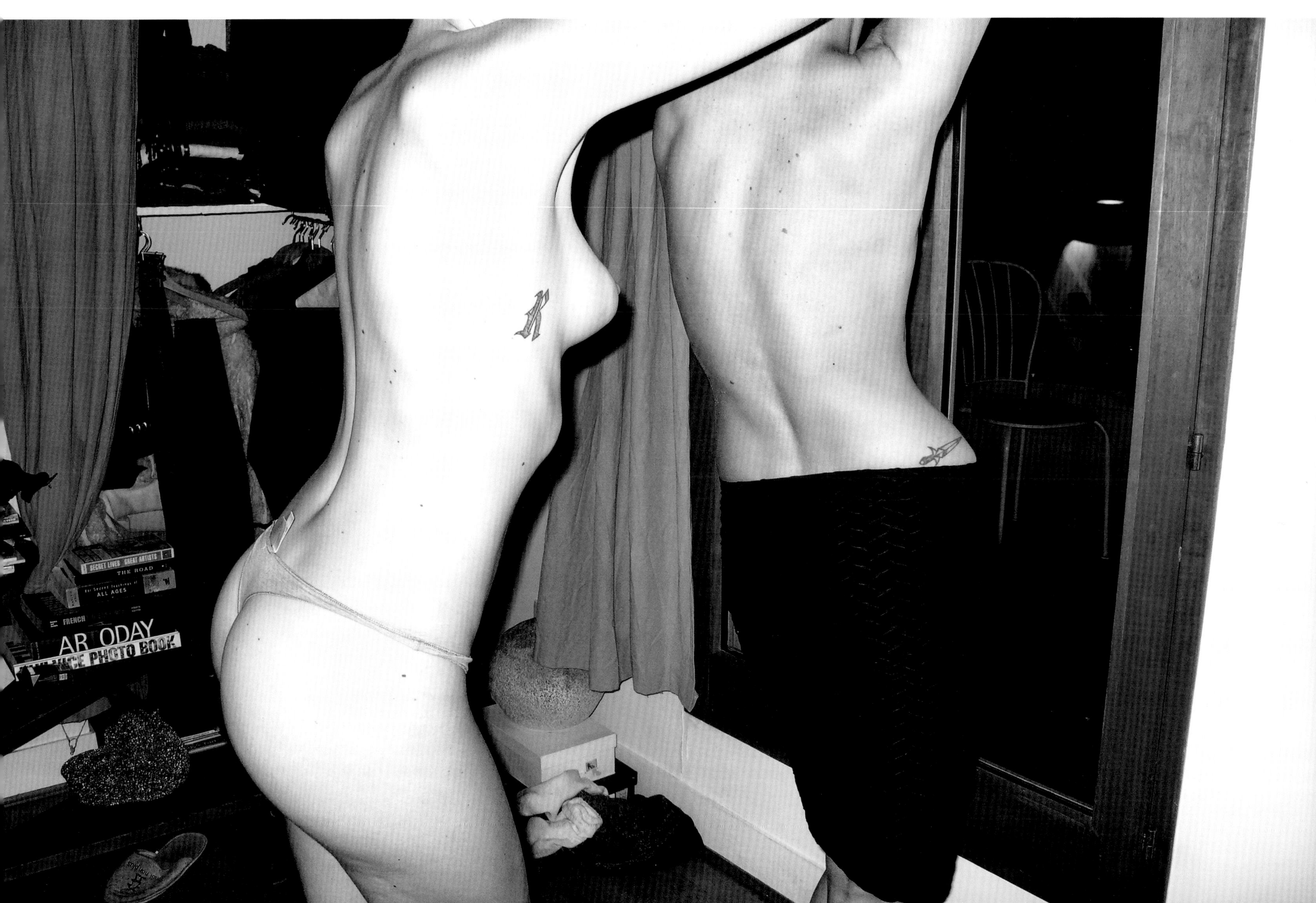

Paris

Prospect Park, New York City

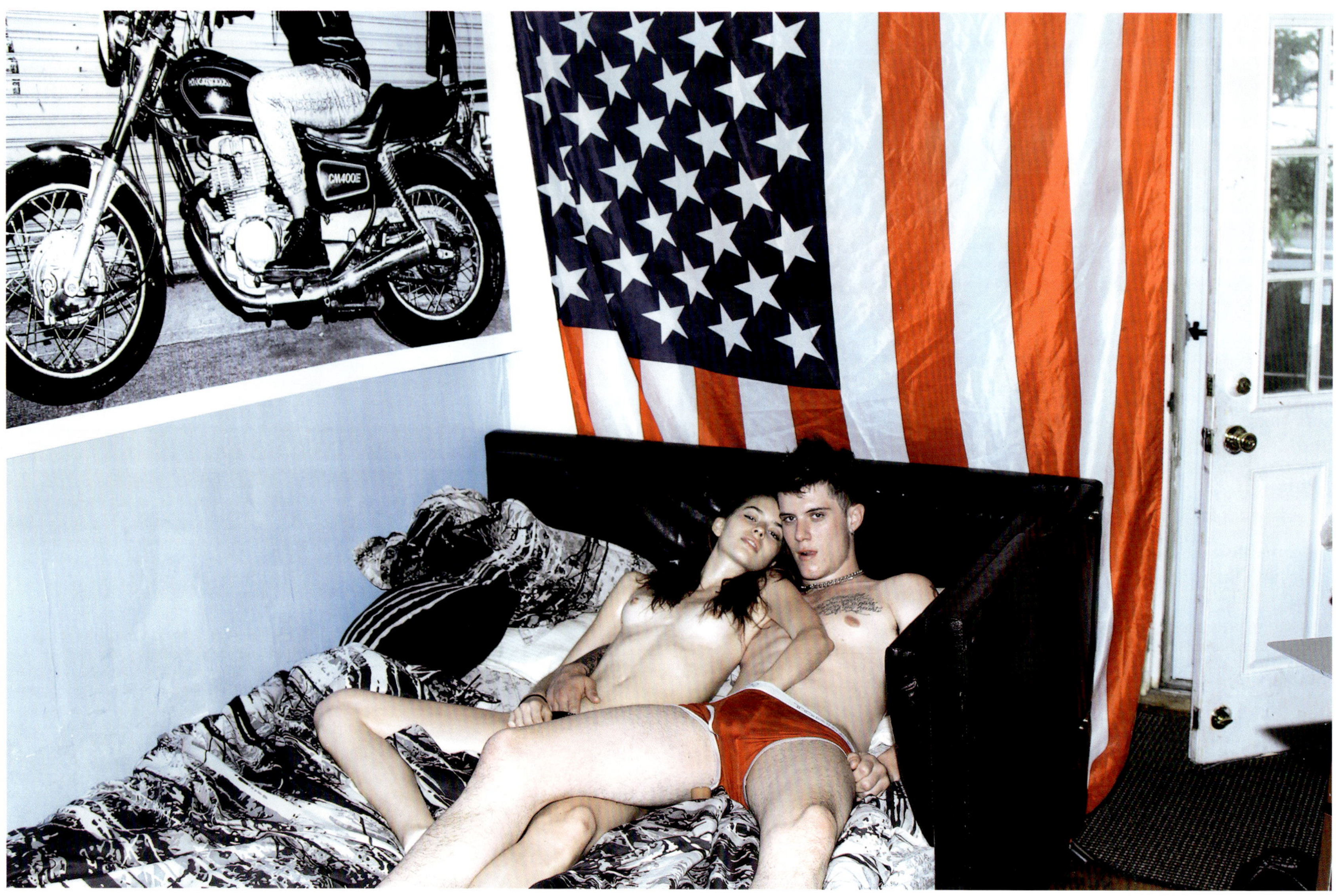

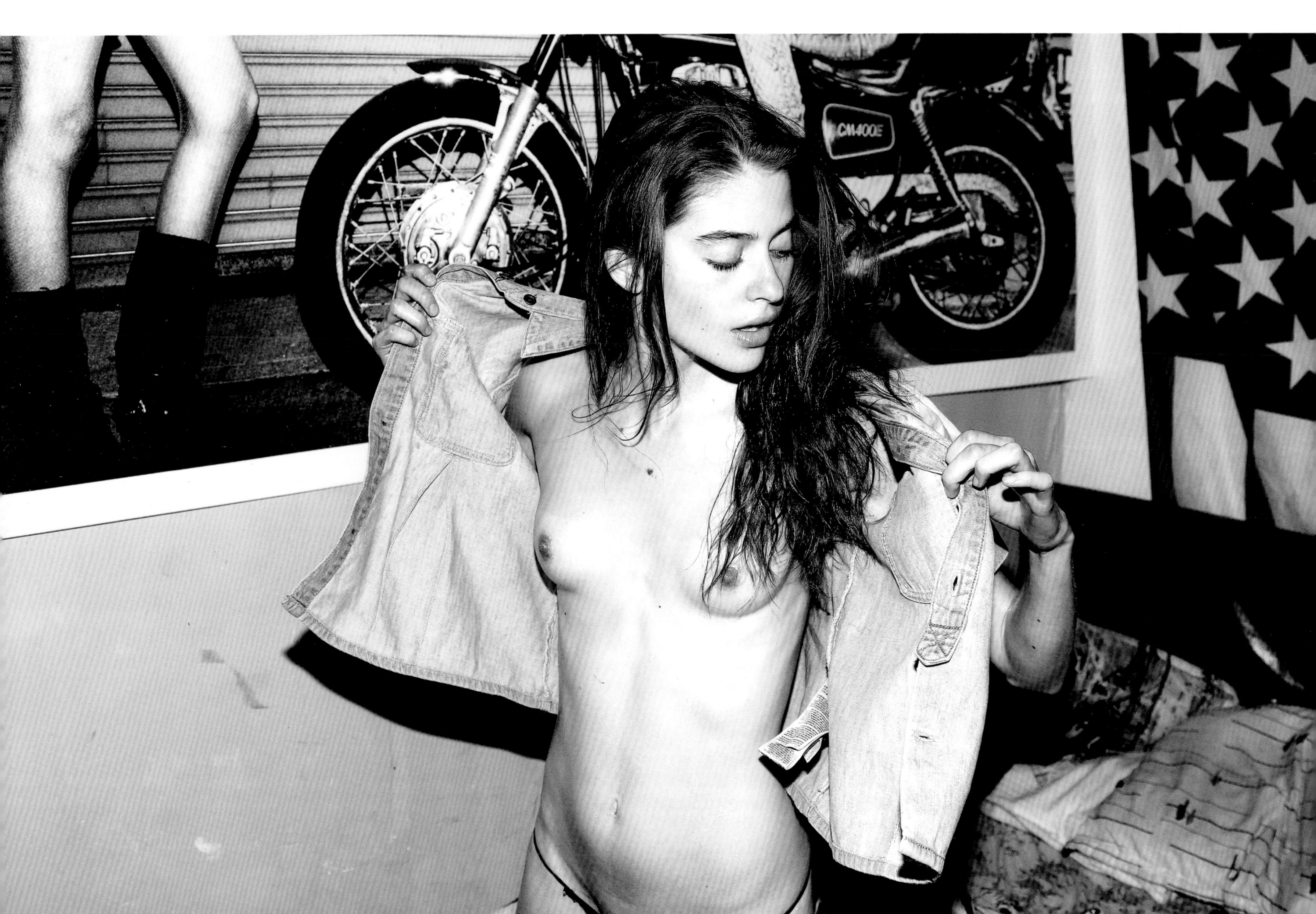

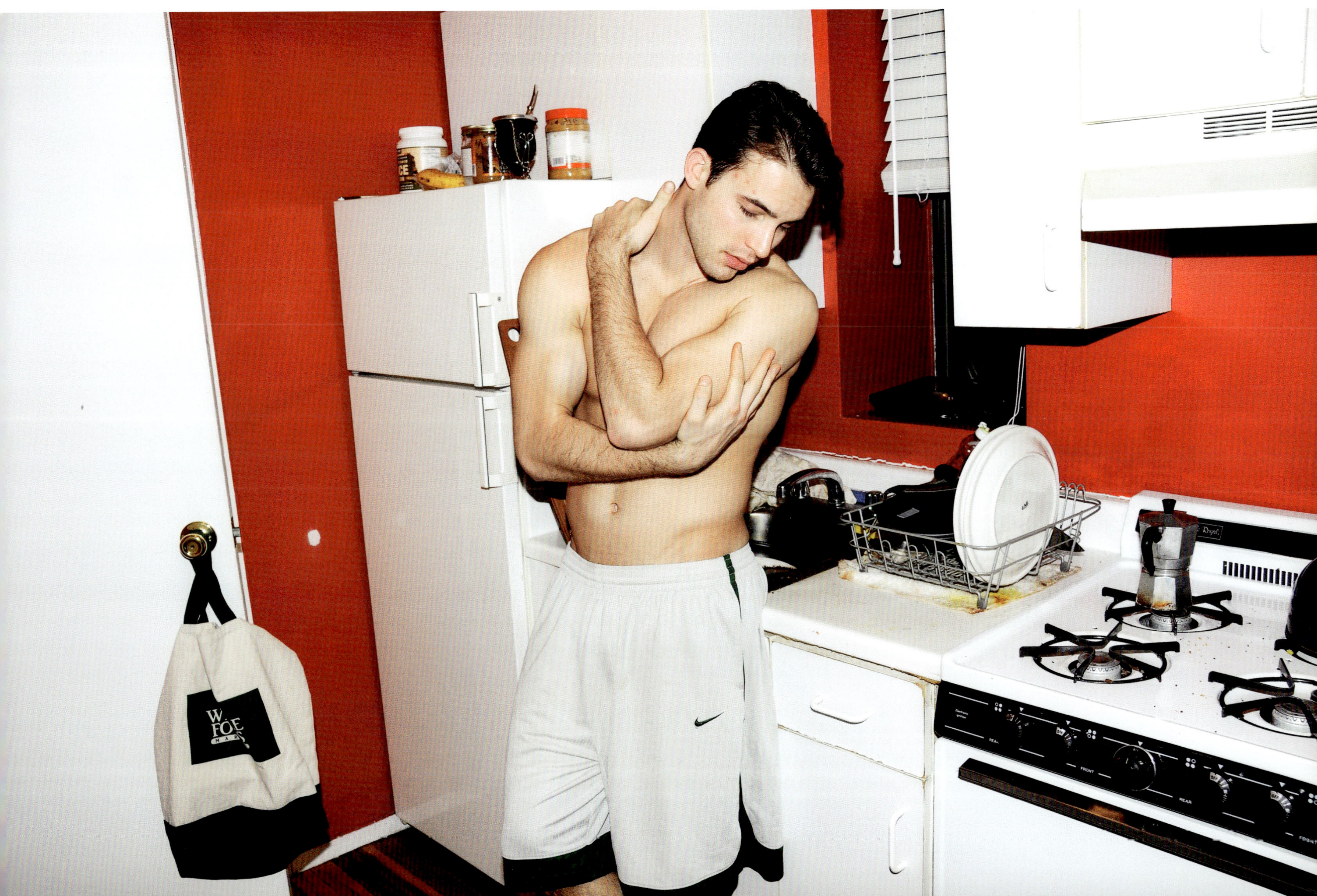

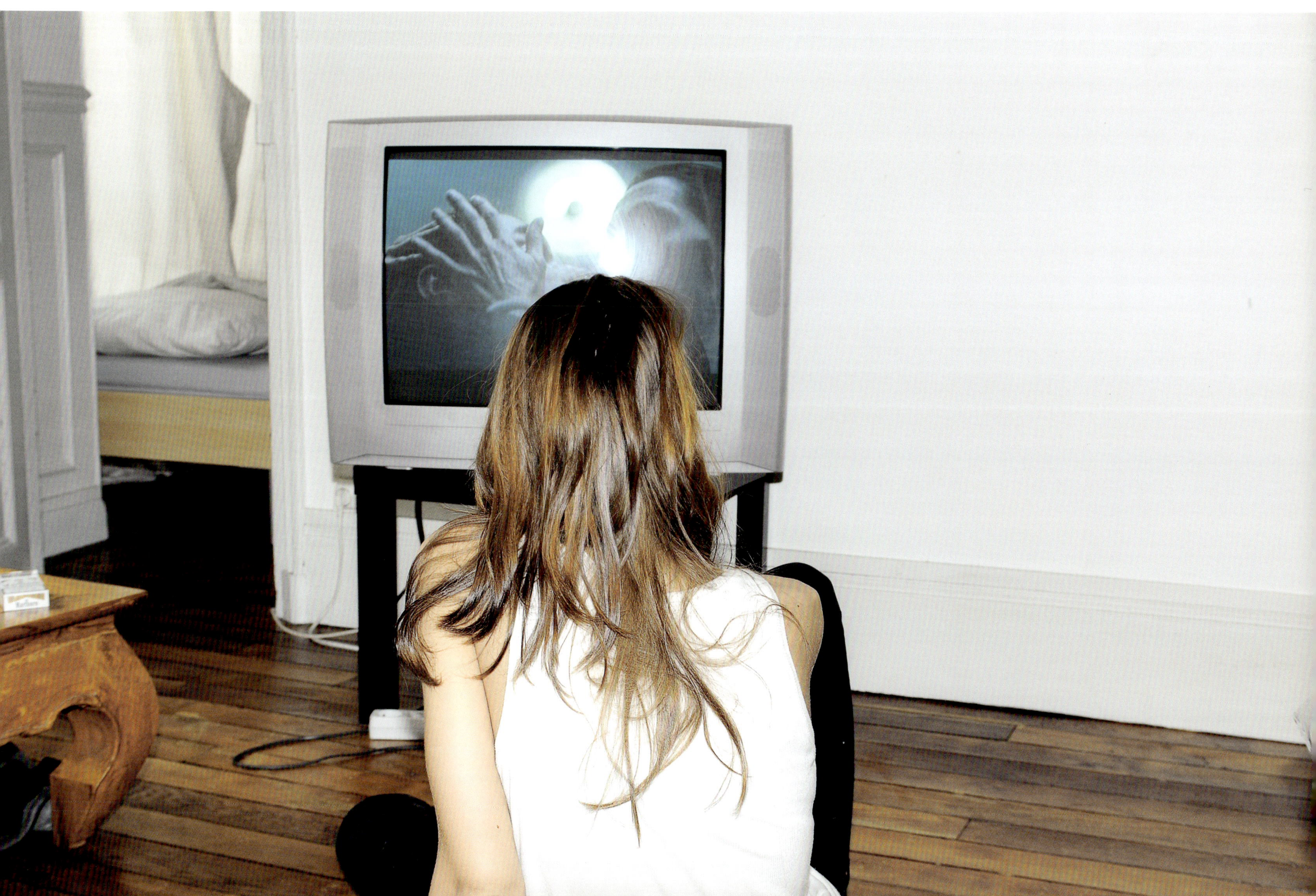

I would like to thank all of the models who allowed me to
enter their private spheres. It has been a privilege and a
revelation on every level.

Special thanks go to Raquel Nave, my friend, muse, and
fellow artist. I could not have completed this book without
the support of William Laven, Nadine Barth, Paul Putzar,
Michael Gross, Stephan Crasneanscki, and Slater Bradley.
I also thank Deborah Culloden, Len Mattson, Samantha
Weaver, Cory Jacobs, Laura Beckwith, Diego Lozano, Jeff
Poe, Magdalena Demaría, Philip Bechtel, Bernhard von
Guretzky, Maya Iseli, Walter Schoenauer, Margaret Klenck,
Milen Till, and Tristan Kabir. Finally, I would like to thank
the staff of *Zeit Magazin* and Hatje Cantz Verlag for making
this project a reality.

Consulting editor: *Nadine Barth*
Copyediting: *Aaron Bogart*
Design: *Paul Putzar*
Project management: *Sonja Altmeppen, Hatje Cantz*
Production: *Franziska Lang, Hatje Cantz*
Reproductions: *Prints Professional*
Printing: *Offsetdruckerei Karl Grammlich GmbH, Pliezhausen*
Paper: *Profisilk, 170 g/m²*
Binding: *Josef Spinner Großbuchbinderei GmbH, Ottersweier*

Published by
Hatje Cantz Verlag GmbH
Mommsenstr. 27
10629 Berlin
Germany
Tel. +49 30 3464678-00
Fax +49 30 3464678-29
www.hatjecantz.com
A Ganske Publishing Group company

Hatje Cantz books are available internationally at selected
bookstores. For more information about our distribution
partners, please visit our website at www.hatjecantz.com.

Printed in Germany
ISBN 978-3-7757-4246-7